THOUGHTS OF GOD

Reflections Before the Desert Storm

And

Poems From the Wilderness of Hope

Angela Dwamena-Aboagye

Copyright © 2011 by Angela Dwamena-Aboagye

Thoughts of God
Reflections Before the Desert Storm and Poems From the Wilderness of Hope
by Angela Dwamena-Aboagye

Printed in the United States of America

ISBN 9781613791820

All rights reserved solely by the author. The author guarantees all contents are original and do not infringe upon the legal rights of any other person or work. No part of this book may be reproduced in any form without the permission of the author. The views expressed in this book are not necessarily those of the publisher.

Unless otherwise indicated, Bible quotations are taken from The Ryrie Study Bible, New King James Version. Copyright © 1985 by Moody Press, Chicago; and The King James/Amplified Parallel Version. Copyright © 1954, 1958, 1962, 1964, 1965, 1987 (Lockman Foundation) by Zondervan, Grand Rapids, Michigan.

www.xulonpress.com

Angela Dwamena-Aboagye heads a non-profit organization she founded in 1995 that works to support survivors of domestic abuse and sexual violence in Ghana. A passionate advocate for empowerment of women and the protection of children from exploitation and abuse, Angela studied to become a lawyer at the University of Ghana and the Ghana School of Law (1984-1989). She also earned a Masters-in-Law Degree from the Georgetown University Law Centre, Washington, D.C, focusing on Women's Legal Rights Studies (1994-1995), and a Master-of-Arts in Theology and Missions from the Akrofi-Christaller Institute, Ghana (2006). Angela fellowships with the Atomic Hills Estates branch of the International Central Gospel Church in Accra, where she is a Deaconess and a Counselor. Married for twenty years to her dear Kwame, they have four lovely children- Freda, Dorsina, Nana Akua and Papa Kwaku.

PREFACE

Since I was a child, I have been, at least most of my life, a rather precocious, somewhat quite confident somebody, or I have been told this so many times I tend to believe it about myself. I have not, generally speaking, been a person prone to anxiety, although I am quite sensitive to cruelty and injustice of any kind. Looking back I realize that I have mostly taken the world as it has presented itself to me, mostly looking at the brighter side of life, and bestowing sunny smiles on people who care to get it from me. I sort of faced challenges the same way, with the attitude that somehow, things would turn out right no matter how dire the situation seemed. Thus I have had my normal run of growing up problems, a few thorny marital issues, and three caesarian sections; hated flying in airplanes, but have done so anyway when the opportunity presented itself, all without much trepidation. Why? Because even before I accepted Christ as my Savior at about age seventeen, (although I must admit that making Him Lord of my life came much later), I always had this sense that God is with me, and all is well with the world– or so it seemed to me.

I've done my fair share of sinning, especially in my youthful years; however, by the great grace of God and His mercy, when I came to faith in Christ and later in life asked Him to be my Lord and Master, I had a great sense of being absolutely loved and cared for. My Father in heaven answered my prayers, even the ones I call my silliest prayers. Backsliding? I have been there too, but God's mercy brought me back to Himself, bringing me to a place of rededication and the desire to live for and walk with Him – for always.

So, I have lived an upbeat life, even in seemingly tough times - until the time a desert storm hit – big time - from mid-2008. Maybe I should have anticipated this storm, having had a tiny inkling of it around age seventeen; but I thought that brief but tormenting experience was long gone, dulled and dimmed in my memory. But this was not to be. The storm this time came with whirlwind, darkness and swirling mists… simply, my world fell apart. Psalm 88, written by Heman, perhaps captures closely my emotional and physical state in this wilderness storm. Described in the notes of the New King James Version of my Ryrie Study Bible as a leader of a choral guild in the time of King David, Heman wrote in verses 13-15 of this sad Psalm, "But to You I have cried out, O Lord… why do You cast off my soul? Why do You hide Your face from me? I have been afflicted and ready to die… I suffer Your terrors; I am distraught." I was floundering, lost and had no clue as to the "why" of the storm, nor how to come back to the land of the living. I forgot that when my world is completely shaken, my God is not shaken, nor can He be shaken off from loving His own. I have captured the story of my life during this period in the Poem below:

But God!

I couldn't eat, I couldn't sleep
I was agitated, I paced up and down
I was giving up totally on myself
I felt worthless, dirty even, impure;
I lost weight so rapidly
I was a wonder to people around me.
My head could not be held up by my neck
Stiffness – a dull pain, a constant ache
I was haunted by strange, surreal dreams
Haunted by a future I could neither see nor hold
I tried to grasp a sense of God, a sense of self
Where had my mind gone? Had I lost it?

Could I ever be Mother again?
Could I be a gentleman's wife?
My clothes hang on my frame
My hair was growing limp,
My mouth, constantly dry.
Frightened, I stared with unseeing eyes
Into the night; night after night.
What was I going to do?
Who would understand me?

Thoughts of God

Who on this earth would help me?
Where was God when I needed Him most?

Detestable, repetitive thoughts,
Unwanted fears, doubts about my identity
All came crushing down on me…
Therapy and drugs could only do so much.

But God!

My God never abandoned me, never let me go
Even when I couldn't feel Him
Even when I thought I'd lost Him
He was there all the time - And still is.
How He has loved me through this all!

I was faithless; He was faithful;
I was fearful, He was faithful;
I was doubtful; still, He was faithful.
He directed me to the Holy Bible -
Literally pulled out verses for me;
He sent angels in human form
So many I can't recount them all;
They spoke to my fevered mind
Words of encouragement, words of peace.
Through my tears, their prayers went up
In all kinds of places, and still do.

I don't know why You love me so, Jesus
It seemed I turned away so many times
Wondering whether You still loved me,
Could hear me, see me, would ever help me.

You did not give up on me – Never.
And I know now, never will You…

Little by little, my strength returned.
When my praise was taken away,
Praise began to fill my mouth again
The clouds in my head began to disappear
Though some remain, I do not fear,
For God is with me – His name is Immanuel!
My stomach can take in food
So much I have to watch my mouth!
I can sing, read, watch a movie with the kids;
Think, sit with people – Praise the Lord!
Though my back hurts at times
And I seem to smell non-existent things
This is my final frontier, for my Redeemer lives –
And whether I die or live, I am His!

He loves me, He loves me
No one can take that away from me –
Neither peril, nor distress
Nor death, depth, height, life
Nor any other created thing
Can take His love away from me.

Father, My Father, I come.
I climb unto Your heavenly lap;
Embrace me in Your loving arms;
Let me lay my tired head on Your breast
Let my soul be at peace like a little child.
I know You have heard me, Lord
Because You truly love me.

I hail You, Father, Jesus and Holy Spirit.
Glory be to Your precious Name!
Marvellous things have You done!

(Written at the waterfront of the Volta Lake at Atimpoku, Ghana, on 19th November, 2009)

It is indeed the love of God and His pure grace that picked me up and saw me through to this point – it is late in 2010 as I write this. Somewhere along this bewildering journey it became clear that what I have experienced has a name after all – Obsessive Compulsive Disorder (OCD), a serious bio-medical, neuro-psychiatric condition – of a spiritual/religious type, also known as "scrupulosity" in Christian circles. With all its attendant miseries (depression, anxiety, etc), it is a condition known to afflict believer and non-believer – although I did not know this from the onset. Nor is OCD restricted to any gender, race or socio-economic group. While there seems to be a dearth of information on this condition in my country Ghana (which is not surprising, since mental health issues are still considered somewhat a taboo subject generally), I have since come to know a few people who have recounted similar experiences that I clearly now know to be OCD or OCD-like conditions. These sufferers require attention, treatment and tons of understanding, especially from family members.

There is documented evidence of believers who suffered OCD, whose work the Christian Church celebrates today, such as John Bunyan, 17th Century

Thoughts of God

preacher and author of the much loved and read "Pilgrim's Progress", Martin Luther (1483 – 1546), the initiator of the Reformation, and Therese of Lisiuex (1873 – 1897), also known as Little Flower, whose work on reaching God through childlike trust in Jesus is celebrated by Catholics the world over. There are other giants in the Lord, who have suffered debilitating depression, a close 'ally' of OCD, such as Charles H. Spurgeon, a fiery 19th Century English preacher, and William Cowper (1731 – 1800), prolific hymn writer, who wrote the song "God moves in a mysterious way…" All this came as a big surprise to me. How on earth can believers suffer this mental condition? But one thing runs through their stories - they each have much to say about the abounding grace of God that took them through these terrible phases of their lives.

There are countless others who have suffered in silence (and are still suffering if alive) because of the shame of admitting one is going through such a hideous trial of the mind. Those who have ventured to speak about it have faced stigma, misunderstanding and even misdiagnosis by professionals and Christian ministers.

So what is the point of this book of *Reflections* (mostly written in my happy days a year or so before the OCD "desert storm" hit), and the *Poems* (penned during the wilderness experience and still being written whenever the inspiration comes)? I want my loved ones and all who read it to know that our adversary, the devil, is on a relentless prowl with his most deadly weapons targeted against believers. OCD and its related disorders (such as Tourette's syndrome), form part of this destructive arsenal. OCD is designed to attack your identity, and your very being and faith in Christ, but if you know this, through God you can gain freedom. What the Bible says is true. Ignorance kills. Knowing next to nothing about OCD almost killed me - but God! The applied Word of God through knowledge can either prevent mental ill-health, or bring healing and restoration to those who must be saved from OCD and other attendant mind attacks and disorders. Comfort, (though it seems far off during such experiences) and renewal are found in the Word for *any* condition. God, through Jesus, has truly loved me through it all. He clung to me when I felt like I was falling off. I am still walking the road to full restoration, but I cannot wait to tell the truth of God's faithfulness. My prayer is that OCD sufferers and their families will NEVER GIVE UP HOPE in any circumstances – no matter what! If the fierce love of God has upheld me through this wilderness and I am living proof of His grace, then you cannot give up. It is well.

I have included an appendix that contains simple explanations of OCD and helpful resources for anyone who needs it – sufferers, families and loved ones of sufferers; pastors, counselors and ministers. God bless you.

Angela

ACKNOWLEDGEMENTS

My gratitude and love to Kwame, my dear husband for his unflinching support and tough encouragement. Though much bewildered, he is certainly grateful to God for my season of restoration; thanks to my children - Freda, Abnaa, Nana Akua and Kwaku - who though not fully understanding, were there in that difficult place with me. I am so grateful for your lives and love.

To my church Pastors, Wiafe Asante, Dickson, Annor, Langdon and Kwame Asare; to Pastors Hammond, Charles and Sam; Abu-Offe, David Asare, and Nkum who I surmise may not have had much of a clue about the nature of my affliction to give it an appropriate label, but whose invaluable prayer support and sensitivity held me up. Thank you all so much and may God grant you more wisdom, love and the heart of the shepherd.

How can I say thanks enough to my wonderful siblings? To be fair to them, I didn't say anything until about six months down the road of suffering, but they rallied to prop me up the moment the cat came out of the bag. To Rosa, Dor (my primary doctor), Krys, Gloria, Patricia (God is faithful, Sis, right?), Emmanuel and Carlos, who in different but loving ways did so much to help me through this bewildering phase of my life.

To the watchwomen and watchmen God stationed all over my walls in prayer and support – my dear sister-in-law Naana, Mama Tess Wiafe Asante, Sisters Dorcas Asare and Pat Adjei, Mrs. Dakwa, Mama Rose Asare, Mama Lu Dickson, Rev. Dorothea, Nana Adwoa Abrefa and Buelah (who's since gone to be with the Lord); Dr. Dakwa, Rev. Akyia, Isaac, Sammy, Michael, Emmanuel, Eric, Chief and many others including my colleagues at work – I am truly grateful for the prayer covering. Continue with me!

To my beautiful Christian therapist, Dr. Ama Edwin, also a "sister-in-arms" – thank you!

To one great 87 year old woman, my mother Rose, who stayed with me one and half years, caring for me with all her heart, prayers, cooking and love - Ma, with tears of gratitude in my eyes I say God Almighty, your Father, be your life and strength.

Finally, I am truly grateful to my friend and Christian sister, Professor Akosua Adomako Ampofo, Senior Researcher, author, and head of the Institute of African Studies, University of Ghana, and my brother Carlos Sakyi, Christian Songwriter and Music Rights Advocate, for reading the draft of this book and giving me invaluable suggestions to improve it. God richly bless you both!

This book is dedicated to my dearest friend Janey
– She knows why.

My whole life I owe to One – Jesus Christ,
to whom all glory belongs!

An Introductory Note to the Reflections and Poems

In late 2007 I was inspired to write some Reflections on various subjects about my Christian life and walk with God, which I shared with friends on my e-mail lists every week for almost a year. The Reflections in this book, apart from one, (titled "The 'Interregnum'"), come from those days. In this book the Reflections have been placed in no particular order, so as to match each one with two Poems selected from a hundred pieces I wrote mostly in 2010 (though a couple were written in 2008 and 2009). The Poems reflect my experience in "the wilderness", as I battled with OCD from mid 2008. Although in writing the Poems my mind was not on the Reflections I wrote in my "happy" days in 2007 and early 2008, I discovered that there was a kind of affinity between the Reflections and many of the Poems, so I matched them in this book. What is the lesson that I gained in this 'strange' affinity? It is this: is it any wonder that in the Book of Philippians, Chapter 3 v. 10, in one line, St. Paul talks about the "power of His resurrection", and the "fellowship of

His sufferings", as the most critical considerations in KNOWING CHRIST?

Reflections One   November 4, 2007

The Thought of God...

I wrote this to tell how I was inspired to do these *Reflections* I have named "Thoughts of God" through a poem recited to me by my then 84 year old Mama. She is now a sprightly 87 year old, with a memory still as sharp as a new blade, and best of all, she loves God to bits! Ma was barely a teenager when she was asked to memorize and spew out this poem in a class test, and she has not forgotten it since. I have still not been able to trace the writer of this piece. However, I fell in love with it, and I hope you will too...

<u>A Thought of God</u>*
The thought of God is like a tree
Beneath whose shade I lie
And watch the fleet of snowy clouds
Sail o'er the silent sky.

It is a thought that ever makes
Life's sweetest smiles from tears
And it is a daybreak to our hopes
A sunset to our fears.

One while it bids the tears to flow
Then wipes them from the eyes
Most often fills our souls with joy
And always sanctifies.

To think of Thee is almost prayer
And is outspoken praise
And pain can even passive thoughts
To actual worship raise.

All murmurs lie inside Thy will
Which are to Thee addressed
To suffer for Thee our work
To think of Thee our rest!

Friends, whoever wrote this*, I thank from the bottom of my heart. I thank God also for my sweet Rose of a Mom who recited this to me. Reflect on this THOUGHT OF GOD, breathe it in...and be blessed!

*(*I since discovered a poem by one Frederick William Faber (1814-1863) on the internet, with the same title, although the poem is longer and the verses are arranged differently from what is quoted above. See http://hymnophile.wordpress.com/category/frederick-w-faber-1814-1863/)*

Who is Like You?

You have magnified Your word,
Above Your own name [1] -
Who would do a thing like that,
When all we mortals care about
Is to protect and project our names?
You are so surprising, Lord,

Thoughts of God

So amazing.
Really Lord, You beat my imagination.

Your glory You will not share with anyone [2] -
Who in their most brilliant magnificence is like You?
And yet when You come to us,
When You manifest Your awesome presence,
We are all bathed with glory;
We bask in Your light and awe;
We are touched by Your power.
You are so surprising, Lord,
So amazing.
Really Lord, You beat my imagination.

We are not like You at all,
Yet You work so we may regain paradise lost.
Created in Your image, jaded by sin,
We don't deserve Your goodness at all.
Yet the Word says You work in us,
To will and to do for Your purpose [3] -
By the sacrifice of Yourself
And the advocacy of Your Spirit.
You are so surprising, Lord,
So amazing.
Really Lord, You beat my imagination!

*(Just thinking about the awesomeness and goodness of God,
inspite of all the woes I'd been through...)*
17th March, 2010

Simply Jesus

I imagine You
Come to me
Into my room
With Your sandaled feet.

I imagine You
Hold my hand
With Your nail scarred hands
Saying 'come.'

I imagine You
Lead with Your rod
Drawing me towards
Green pastures.

I imagine You
Hold Your staff
Sitting with me
By quiet waters.

I imagine You
With me sitting at Your feet
Listening to Your words
Bringing me life.

I imagine You
Walking with me
In the garden of Eden
Created for me.

I imagine You
In Your simplicity
Awesome King of Kings
Dying for me.

I imagine You
Rising from the Table
Head of the universe
Serving me. [4]

O what simplicity
Inspiring awesome reverence
Lord of the Universe
Man of Galilee!

Reflections Two October 20, 2007

He aims to transform...

Walking this journey with Christ, I believe I have often told myself, "I have to change." Then as I keep on walking with Him, I gain assurance from the Word and say to myself: "I will change", because His Word says so. "For those He foreknew... He also destined from the beginning to be molded into the image of His Son..." (Romans 8:29 AMP). Then I keep on walking with Him, and then - surprise, surprise! Me, Angela, I am changing!!! It is s-l-o-w, sometimes painfully so; but through His transforming grace, I AM CHANGING! My thoughts, my actions, my reactions, even my smiling! Same old face though, but a different 'inner' countenance...

"...for it is God who is all the while effectually at work in you... both to will and to work for His good pleasure and satisfaction and delight." Philippians 2: 13 AMP

Me? Change? And little by little, step by step, become more like Christ? Really? Yes! Yes! Yes! I am, and I will.
Aren't you amazed?

The Context is the Contest

I said I will change,
Become more like Christ
Day by day as I walk with Him.
I said so, very sure because
His word says so and so it would be.
But the enemy would not have it;
He heard it and said, "We'll see,
Whether her wish will come to pass."
He threw the spokes in my wheel,
With intent to destroy the purpose of God.

For a moment it seemed my wheels stopped turning;
For a moment my feet stopped running;
For a moment destiny stopped to watch;
For a moment I was caught unawares -
Then the great contest began.

My Father was beside Himself;
He said "I'll pant, I'll gasp like a woman in labor; [5]
I'll go after My child, I gave My Son for her;
I'll not give her up, no, I'll never."
My God was simply unstoppable.

The enemy thought he had me
Arrested, broken, shipwrecked;
My Father waited a bit to see
What I'd do in the middle of the track.
"Would she hold on, still believe
That I'll get her, won't let her go?"

I was confused; turned round and round
Seemingly in circles of defeat;
But my loving Father, simply unstoppable,
Saw in me a glimmer of hope;
Looking up, though being sucked in,
He saw my struggles, saw my tears;
Crying out for mercy, knew my fears.

Then said He, "I've seen enough, I'm going after her,"
It was His mercy that brought Him near;
Love that would not let go, love so dear.
He flew in on the wings of the wind;
Came to where I was in the miry clay
And drew me gently, with bands of love.

"How can I let you go, daughter?
I died for you, I live for you;
I swore by myself that you are Mine;
I have redeemed you - return to Me; [6]
I am here child; just put your hand in Mine.

The enemy pushed, the enemy pulled;
He orchestrated, he strategized more;
He swore that he wouldn't let me be,
But he did not know Father has plans for me;
Plans of life, to bring me to His expected end.[7]

The context is the Contest,
In the spirit realms, for my destiny.
My God has declared and it is written -
"You are Mine, and I love you eternally."[8]

Written in the indelible ink,
Of the Savior's own precious blood.

My sins paid for, my soul forgiven,
What could the enemy do with someone like me?
His huffs and his puffs were all in vain;
He could do nothing but let me go;
Vanquished he turned away, tail between his legs.

Caught in my Father's arms, learning to rest,
To bounce back, recuperate, start running again;
Wondering what on earth happened here -
Wondering what the lessons are;
Listening quietly to His heartbeat;
Basking in His love, just sheltering.

I'm learning to run again, testing my strength;
But I know I can do nothing by myself;
In His strength, I live, and have my being;
Nothing more do I want, nothing less -
Enough to know my Father came,
Came and got me back to Him.

In Transit and Transformation

A bondslave to Christ, yet free;
An unprofitable servant, yet valued;
Wounded, yet healed;
Battered, yet built up;
Poor in heart, yet rich in God;
Barren, yet with many children;

Desolate, yet inhabited;
A wilderness, yet like Eden;
A desert, yet like the Lord's garden;
A shipwreck, yet anchored.

That's me, in transformation -
One, yet the other.
That's me, in salvation -
Treading the narrow path
That leads to the door of life,
Haltingly but surely;
Transiting across the realms
In it, but not of it [9]
Towards that land of light -
The place of my fondest dreams.

9th March, 2010

Reflections Three   November 26, 2007

A Matter of the Heart...

Jesus. He must be THE object of my affection. How my heart responds to Him is indicative of how I think of Him. If He is the heart of the matter, then my worship of Him must be a matter of the heart, my heart. My whole life, outlook, perceptions, reality, dreams and ambitions must be about Him. If they are not, then I must examine my heart. He must occupy the core, and fill the whole! He must increase, and I must decrease. I want it no other way, because really, what is my life about without Him, the source of all life? How does this life make sense without Him who makes meaning of it? It was the author Rick Warren [10] who said something to the effect that worship is not singing one or two slow songs and getting that "woozy" feeling of floating in the 'heavenlies' (all special effects mine); *worship is a lifestyle*; and I have no argument about that at all. I am striving for this lifestyle, but thank God for the grace that enables me from day to day, because I cannot do it without His grace.

This is the prayer of my heart: *"Jesus, be the centre... be the fire in my heart; be the wind in these sails; be the reason why I live..."** It's still a song, Lord, but please listen to my heart.

'And in a loud voice they sang: "Worthy is the Lamb who was slain, to receive power and wealth and wisdom and strength and honor and glory and praise!"'
Revelation 5:12 NKJV

Is He not worth all of my worship and my life?

(*Lyrics in a song written by Michael Frye, © 1999 Vineyard Song)

First Love*

I return to You, my First Love
You are my First Love
Return me to You, Lord
For I come, voluntarily
With my will, my heart
My soul and my mind
You alone can satisfy
You alone can quench my thirst
You alone can fill my dryness.

I return to my First Love
I return, my Bridegroom
Your banner over me is love [11]
Purest love, unquenchable fire
It's only You Christ
I return, Lord, I return.

Take me home with You, my Love
Raise Your banner over me
Spread Your wings over me
Cover me with Your lovely hand
Let all anxiety flee
Let my beating breast lie still

Let it lie in the bosom of my love
My First and only love.

I'll talk with You, Lord
I'll walk with You
I'll run to You
Just to be in Your embrace
My Love, my Lord, my First Love.
Christ.

(*Jesus chides the Church of Ephesus for leaving their first love in Revelation Chapter 2 v. 4. I wrote this to tell Jesus that the last thing I want to do is leave is my First Love– Him…)
23rd March, 2010

Hosea's Bride*

I was undesirable,
Yet You married me;
Pledged Your love;
Sacrificed everything for me.

I fled, not even knowing why;
You could have put me away,
But You came after me -
You did not mind my shame.

Uncovered, You covered me
With the blanket of Your love;
Held my hand, led me home,
Back to You, where I belong.

Thoughts of God

Many times the wilderness calls -
Confusion and perplexity;
But You break through my thoughts,
With gentle whispers of Your love.

My love is not enough,
But You pour in Your love to fill me up;
You keep me at Your side;
Your gentleness has drawn me.

It's only You O Lord,
Who will stick to one like me
And work, until You change me,
Mold me into a beautiful bride.

You are worthy my Husband,
Of all my adoration and worship;
Worthy because of who You are,
Worthy because of what You do.

For You have sworn by Yourself,
That the mountains may be removed,
And the hills may depart -
Your covering of love You'll not remove. [12]

I love You Lord, my Husband;
And O I am still learning
To stay, to trust, to love
Until our love is fully fulfilled.

(Just overwhelmed by the love of God for one like me…and a deep desire to reconnect…*The Poem is based on the Biblical

account of the marriage of the prophet Hosea to an unfaithful woman in the Book of Hosea)
23rd March, 2010

Reflections Four November 17, 2007

The Heart of the Matter...

Jesus. He is not only the centre of the Gospel; He *is* the Gospel. All Scriptures point to Him, and all Scriptures must point to Him. Add everything up - Jesus. Reduce everything - Jesus. Shake things together - Jesus. Let things fall apart - Jesus. In John 5 v. 39, He told the Jewish authorities who were seeking to kill Him: "You search the Scriptures, for in them you think you have eternal life; and these are they which testify of Me." Every attribute or description of this awesome Person you can think of cannot capture the total essence of who He is - all Love, all Good, all Gracious, all Wonderful, all Life, all Mighty, all Healer, all Peace, all Terrible, all Gentle, all Light, all Resurrection, all I AM... Please add to the list. Truth is, no language can contain Him; no numbers of pages of great books can contain Him; even the heavens cannot contain Him! **God** come down! Since I begun to understand this, and I'm still in the process of understanding and knowing this One, as complex as life is, it has become much simpler. A paradox? Maybe. But that is my reality, because no matter the twists and turns of life, all I'll ever need is in Him. And I'm still in the process of discovering...

"In Him we live and move and have our being..." Acts 17: 28

Dear friend, come and walk with me on this road of discovery...

The Joy of the Battle

How could I have recognized
The King on His white horse
With blazing eyes and bronzed feet [13]
If I had not met Him in the battle?

With all the angels in attendance
He would have been a stranger
Perhaps a far-away Savior
Come to take me home for mercy's sake.

But I met Him in the battle
He had gone ahead of me
With the Sword of the Spirit in His hand
He scattered the enemy to the left and right.

He is the Captain of Israel's hosts
A wounded General, a risen Savior
Oseadeeyo, Osaahene, Osagyefo*
He commanded, and the armies stood still.

Who is this General who fights
With His eye on His struggling soldiers
With one blast the enemy scatters
And He turns to carry His wounded to safety?

Sometimes Captain leaves me to fight
"Fight on", He shouts, "never give up!
I have trained your hands for battle [14]
Use them in My Name, you have the power!"

But never is He far away from me
He brings water out of rocks when I thirst
He makes oases in deserts so I can rest
And when I sleep, He watches over me.

The enemy is mad, he re-strategizes
"Why should she get what should be mine?"
He forgets I have been ransomed
By the General, Captain of Israel's armies.

My General bids me never to fear
He says, "When you are afraid, trust in Me;
I am the Lord of the battle, of the fight
You have seen the works of the arm of the Lord."

Even without the angels my Captain can fight
The all-powerful deliverer, all-sufficient God!
Who is like unto Him, to whom shall we liken him?
Captain of Israel's hosts, Lord of the battle!

So fierce has been the battle of my life
I've fallen many times, wounded, tired
But this Captain, so loving, so gentle
Never gave up on me, never sent me off.

The arm of the Lord has gloriously triumphed [15]
His blood on the Cross is my defense

Strong tower and mighty fortress
Lord of the battle, Living Savior.

Will a battle ever be sweet?
Yes, and only when you know who leads
Yes, when you know who saves
Yes, when you know victory is sure.

So trudge on my sister, march on, my brother
Through the mud and the stormy rain
At every step the Captain is next to you
In darkness, valleys, danger or in pain.

The General's name is a strong tower
You run into it, completely safe [16]
Know His name, know His power
Know His covenant forever stands.

The enemy's army will turn against itself
One by one, his units will fall
Oh, they will assemble, but they will fall [17]
So says His Word, Captain of my salvation.

How I love You, Jesus my General
I come to you in faith, I come with words
Believing, trusting, hoping and knowing
The Lord of the Battle will always fight for me!

(In the Akan language of Ghana, **Oseadeeyo** means 'He who does what He says'; **Osaahene** means 'the King of the battle'; and **Osagyefo** portrays a 'Warrior-savior.')*
9th April, 2010

There's Something About Jesus

There's something about Jesus -
Riveting,
Unforgettable,
Starkly simple,
Pure.

There's something about Jesus -
So different,
Human,
Absolutely divine,
Together.

There's something about Jesus -
Humility's height,
Divinity's delight,
Love's expression,
Night's light.

There's something about Jesus -
Sure Rock,
Gentle Lamb,
Son of Man,
God.

Reflections Five   January 17, 2008

The Blessing of Abraham

We find in the Bible a fascinating profile of the man Abraham, alias *Friend of God!* God Almighty Himself called him "My friend". [18] What a testimony. Will that be said of me too one day? To me, that is what the Blessing of Abraham is about. That close relationship; that intimacy between two persons; the surprising element being that One is a Transcendent, *Utterly Other* Being, and the other a mere mortal. What distinguished Abraham? It seems without doubt it was his faith - here meaning putting his trust absolutely in a God his fathers and mothers had not known. In Genesis 15 v. 6, we are told "… (Abraham) believed God, and it was accounted to him for righteousness." Because God said so, that was it. But on this journey there were many crises and a great testing. It was no little thing for a godly man to ask his wife to tell a half-truth that she was his sister, for fear of a powerful ruler who lusted after her; [19] and I cannot fathom how he managed to hold on to his sanity when to test him Jehovah asked him to kill and burn his only heir and son Isaac as sacrifice to Him (God).[20] Abraham also engaged in serious military battles in the desert against enemies, [21] but all the while, there was God. He was never far away from Abraham, no matter the circumstances - talking to him, revealing His plans, eating with him, letting Abraham know his every big or little move mattered to Him. And Abraham *knew God's voice!* And oh, what great grace, favor, anointing and honor were upon Abraham. Was he a perfect man? No. But once God sets His love upon you, He doesn't let go until He has perfected that which concerns you. Just as He did for Abraham.

"Therefore know that the LORD your God, He is God, the faithful God who keeps covenant and mercy for a thousand generations with those who love Him and keep His commandments..." Deuteronomy 7: 9 (NKJV)

I want to be God's friend. Infact if that is all I get written on my tombstone when I'm gone and it's God's testimony of me, that'll be more than enough. The Blessing of Abraham would be mine too. Just think about it.

You Are Able

I won't fail You,
Because You won't fail me.
You are the God who works in me,
Both to will and to do for Your pleasure.[22]
You have the roadmap for me,
The straight and narrow road,
Which by Your Blood,
You have set me on;
Which by Your love,

Thoughts of God

You will keep me on;
And by Your grace,
I'll run the race;
Run to the finish.

Sometimes I feel the world,
Is coming apart around me;
But it's only a feeling,
Not the real thing;
The truth is You.
You made an eternal covenant,
By Your own mercies,
For Your own name's sake,
With me, when You saved me;
I did nothing,
You did everything,
And swore by Yourself
To keep me till the very end.

I have no real cause
To fear or be anxious
About what God does;
To accomplish His purpose.
Mine is to trust,
Mine is to rest,
Mine is to know,
He loves too deeply
To simply let go.
Jesus bids me leave
My burdens at the Cross,
Because He's big enough,
To carry and to bear.

So I come O Lord,
So foolish I am,
I just thank You
That You know me so well.
Do not hold it against me, Lord,
I do believe in You.
Help me to trust more,
Help me to know
That You help the helpless,
And that I can't help You
To do Your sovereign will.
The beauty of it all is,
You can and You will.
               Amen.

25th April, 2010

Faith and Trust

Faith is the great knowing;
Trust is the great holding.
Faith begins; Trust sticks -
When there's no showing.
Faith comes with a big bang;
Trust is rather quiet...
Together, they are dynamite!

15th March, 2010

Reflections Six   October 2010

The 'Interregnum'*

"And Sarah laughed"; we are told in Genesis Chapter 18 v. 12, upon hearing that God was ready to give her husband Abraham and herself, both almost a century old, the long promised child. It was the laughter of unbelief… how on earth was God going to do this using her almost no good reproductive system? But God did not give up on her, because God is faithful to His word. Fast forward to the New Testament–the Book of Hebrews, Chapter 11 v.11, where it is written: "By faith Sarah received strength to conceive seed… because she judged Him faithful who had promised…" What happened to Sarah in the 'interregnum'? What translated her from the laughter of unbelief to the laughter of faith? I surmise that Sarah remembered where she had come from and where she had been, with Abraham – through it all. She remembered what God had done, protecting her from lustful kings when in two instances, out of fear, Abraham asked her to lie to foreign rulers that she was his sister, not his wife; [23] God forgiving her interference in His divine process to give Abraham an heir of the promise when she gave her maid servant Hagar to him so they could have a child through her (Hagar); [24] and God's covering in times of danger and war in the desert. [25] Sarah *remembered* God's faithfulness to her husband – not giving up on him when he messed up big time. She remembered that inspite of all these things, God had never failed in His friendship and faithfulness to them; God called and treated Abraham as His friend! He had not altered His word to them… and best of all, He looked beyond their faults, and saw their need of Him for their salvation, sustenance and fulfillment. From laughter in unbelief, Sarah walked towards the light of faith, and received strength through faith to conceive and bear a child in a seemingly hopeless situation. The laughter of unbelief turned into the laughter of a promise received – her own Isaac! Now she is in the annals of history and celebrated in the 'Hall of Faith' in the Book of Hebrews as a giant of faith! She got there through grace and God's own faithfulness by which He doesn't give up on His children in their own crisis or trial of faith; who gives them another chance and nurtures them back to Himself as they also turn to Him for His help – crying out in earnest and honesty – "Lord, I believe, help my unbelief." (Mark 9 v. 24). God knows we believe He is, that He is able to do anything, but we are struggling with our human limitations, the opposition of the world and the enemy's attacks. God reaches out and strengthens us, drawing us by His lovingkindness… I believe that is what happened to Sarah in the interregnum. If God did not give up on Sarah, He won't give up on me. Faith is also a gift. Ask, and it shall be given. Lord, I believe You for everything today and beyond… help my unbelief!

"Let us hold fast the confession of our hope without wavering, for He who promised is faithful." (Hebrews 10:37)

(*An interregnum is described as a period between two reigns or governments of a country. I used the word to symbolize the transformation of Sarah, between her self-rule and God's rule over her life, eventually earning her a place in the New Testament as a mother of faith. This Reflection is the only one in this book written during my "wilderness" period, when I knew I was slowly but surely recovering from OCD and "finding faith" [26] *again.)*

Grace and Faith

Grace and Faith are twins,
One cannot be without the other;
Grace delivered me to Faith,
And Faith delivered me to Christ.

So I came to Christ in Faith through Grace;
In Christ, Grace has sustained me in Faith;
For at the lowest ebb of Faith,
Grace carried me and saw me through.

Because of Grace, God remains faithful,
For He cannot be unfaithful
To His word – Grace upon Grace,
Grace that is greater than all my sin.

Thank You God for Grace;
And thank You God for Faith;

Both for me and both with me -
Never one without the other!

7th March, 2010

Waiting

God.
Who gives power to the weak
And increases strength
To those who have no might
To them that wait upon Him.

Who says running is easy,
And walking is light?
Yet He says, "You will walk
And not be weary;
You'll run, and not faint!"[27]
But He is able to make this possible
For He is God, in us.

And waiting - comes in many shades -
Waiting can be light and joyful;
Or in anguish and pain;
Waiting can be baffling,
Also in hope and faith -
For an hour, a day,
A week or months -
Even for many years.

But the promise is sure;
They that wait on the Lord,
Shall renew their strength.
The real wonder is that
God actually waits for us,
To come and wait on Him.
How He longs to bless us!
How He patiently waits
For wayward ones to come
And receive His abundant grace.

Lord, as we come to wait,
Let us be still before You;
Let us enjoy Your presence;
Let us listen to Your voice;
In stillness and in quietness.
Light up our darkness;
Still the storms in our hearts;
And let us rise up from our knees,
Still waiting as we go;
Waiting as we walk;
Waiting as we run.
Amen.

Reflections Seven   13th May, 2008

The Sound of Silence…

Isn't it somewhat disconcerting for a child of God when God seems quiet for a period of time? I don't know what your experience is, friend, but there are times when I don't seem to hear Him, feel Him or see a tangible move of His in my life, for a while. Oh, but only for a while. Because I'm learning quite fast that when God is about to do something, there seems to be a period of stillness; a "disconnect" of a sort. Sometimes I pray, but I feel as though my words just bounced off the walls of my room; that deeply satisfying feeling I used to get after communing with my Father in heaven just seems not to be there. But dear friend, this is no disconnect– it's a call to draw deeper into Him, to hold on for dear life, to repeat His promises over and over to myself – to walk, practically, by faith. It's a time to tell *Abba*, my Father, that I'm desperate for Him, that I need another touch, a fresh anointing, a renewal by His Spirit. In Psalm 63 v.1b-2, David said it so clearly: "My soul thirsts for you, my flesh longs for you in a dry and thirsty land where there is no water. So I have looked for You in the sanctuary, to see Your power and Your glory." The truth is, Jesus *never* leaves us, nor forsakes us, therefore in such "dry" periods He hasn't gone anywhere; He's just drawing me in slowly but surely into the inner sanctuary, pleading that I discern more clearly and follow the still, small voice that would take me to another level in Him…

"Deep calls unto deep at the noise of Your waterfalls..."
Psalm 42:7a (NKJV)
"...In quietness and confidence shall be your strength."
Isaiah 30:15 (NKJV)

Hold on friend. Change is coming.

Triple Jeopardy* 28

The Lord loved him
He was His dear friend
Yet he got sick
And the Lord seemed hidden
Two days of silence
Two days of waiting

The Lord loved him still
And yet he died
From bad it went to worse
The Lord was still hidden
But He knew everything
Even the sparrow's fall

Sickness and death
Inexplicable distresses
Allowed and outworked
For the glory of God?
Yes, that is the Master's plan
Who works His counsel to will

So the Master came
As He always does
The Mighty One in our midst
To seek, to save, to raise
To show we are truly His
In any and all circumstances

Whether in the valley of shadows
Or in cages of iron and bronze
Buried, rotting in stone cold tombs
Bound in triple jeopardy
He loves still in dark places
As He loves in the light

So my Savior comes
To deliver His beloved
From places of captivity
Webs of entanglement
Never ever late
His glory to display

So we wait in expectancy
With patience and quiet hope
Or in desperate cries of mercy
Holding on– our Redeemer lives!
He is mighty in our midst
He will come and save!

(*Based on the story of the death and miraculous raising of Lazarus of Bethany recorded in John 11: 1-44)
4th October, 2010

Speaking In Silence

The same God who spoke over my life
In times past, of praise, glory and joy
Is the same God who speaks now, in silence.

The God of Joseph, of dreams of greatness
Spoke in the pit, in silence. [29]

The God of Jeremiah, lifting him to prophetic prominence
Spoke in the prison, in silence.[30]

The God of Daniel, of heights in captivity
Spoke in the lions' den, in silence.[31]

The God of Ruth, in marital bliss
Spoke in the fields, in silence.[32]

He is ever present, this God of mine
Faithful in joy, faithful in sorrow
Faithful in gladness, faithful in tears
Never changes, never forgets.
In the stillness of silence, hear His voice
The very sound of silence says to you –
"I am here, child, I AM [33] is here."

June, 2010

Reflections Eight   September 24, 2008

He Knows, He Understands...

Sometimes the child of God goes through an experience that leaves her "flabberwhelmed' and "overghasted", as a friend of mine used to say. It's such an experience that it leaves you wondering- "what on earth happened here"? I don't know about you, but there's a tendency to think that even God has been taken by surprise by the particular experience. I am currently struggling with something I simply don't understand – in my mind. Intrusive words and images in my mind I simply detest and cringe to speak out loud. Mind boggling and strange; frightening even, because it is as though I can't control or suppress these thoughts and images. Inspite of being in this very difficult place as a child of God, I am learning, oh, I am learning, that absolutely nothing takes our God by surprise. He knows. He sees it coming. He knows the exact time it'll hit. BUT GOD! He has already prepared a way out for His child, and He is faithful to the end. Have you felt that lately? That He couldn't have known? That He just doesn't understand this? That if He does, then what is He doing about it??? I have. But take heart my friend. His weapon is sharper than a two-edged sword; it cuts through and cuts apart. His strategies are mighty in Himself for the pulling down of any and all kinds of strongholds. And His peace is like nothing the world gives.

Nothing ever fazes my God. Nothing outwits Him. ***Says the Lord:***

"You whom I have taken from the ends of the earth... You are My servant, I have chosen you and have not cast you away; fear not, for I am with you; be not be dismayed, for I am your God. I will strengthen you; yes, I will help you. I will uphold you with my righteous right hand. " Isaiah 41: 9-10 (NKJV)

Take heart my soul, for the Lord is on your side!!!

The Garrison

Seventy times I asked,
Where are You Lord?
Why don't You see me?
Why don't You hear me?
Where is Your mercy?
Where is Your love?
Do You see my tears?
Do You hear my groans?
Do You see my fears,
My sorrow and woe?

All I felt was silence,
All I heard was quiet;
But I would not shut up,
I cried out some more;
I lay awake at night,

Pleading His Blood and mercy;
Then I remembered,
Clearly and succinctly,
That Father said He would speak,
He would never let me go.

Said He'll speak through nature;
Speak through His written word;
Speak through my daily work;
Speak through good friends;
Speak through my circumstances.
Never silent, always listening,
Never absent, always hearkening;
Drawing me, lifting me
Out of the darkness, out of night,
Into the brightness, into His light.

Remembrance brought hope,
Long hidden, buried under rubble;
The rubble of confusion,
Anxiety, depression and pain.
Hope rose, bidden by an Unseen Hand;
Faith burst forth, budding again;
Love lifted me over the wall;
And where was Peace?
In the grave, lying still,
Waiting for resurrection.

Peace had no choice -
I was laying down burdens at the Cross.
As the burdens fell one by one,
Sometimes left there

Sometimes picked up again,
Christ still bid me come:
"Leave them, daughter,
You can't bear them;
Not only will I bear them,
I'll give you a reward."

"You will see My hand;
You will know My love;
Joy and rejoicing will come,
Thanksgiving and melody;
The desert will grow cedars;
The wilderness will become lush;
Baca will turn into pools of water, [34]
Blessings will abound.
I'll wipe your tears you'll see;
Peace is coming, Peace is here."

I lifted my eyes and behold,
Peace was clad from head to toe,
In great shiny armor; feet asunder.
In her hand were many swords;
Each shining, glistening with the Blood.
She drew near my head, peering close;
She gave the order, "Mount the garrison!"
The swords went up and went around,
Round about my brain, round my head;
"Peace be still!" went up the shout.

The garrison was mounted,
But it was not yet done.
Peace bent down, near my heart -

"Dear, what have we here?" she asked,
"Many tears, bruises and brokenness?"
"Mount the guard!" Went up the cry;
Up went the swords, so many, so sharp;
Round about my heart they went,
Clipped into place, firm and strong.
"Work is done, Sir, the battle's won!"

Jesus looked at me and smiled,
"Do you see me now, Little Flock?
My heart breaks to see you cry,
When I'm so near and love so much.
My Peace I give you, My Peace I leave,
Not as the world gives, do I give;
You will face battles, troubles and tears,
But never fear, I'm always near.
Remember You have My Hope and Love,
You have Faith too, I know you do."

"So go on, wipe those tears,
The garrison is up, have no fears;
Peace is as strong as a thousand
And Peace is going nowhere.
When the billows roll in,
Just be still and remember
That I am the Lord of the waves
And I am King of the floods.
In remembering, Peace will come;
Without you realizing, she'll steal on you."

"Quietly in My bosom you shall rest,
Among the flowers though there are thorns;

I'll keep you safe upon the shore;
There's nothing to fear anymore;
You are Mine, the love of My heart;
You are honored and very loved.
Know that always, My dear,
That's your clue to victory.
And this is for sure, for certainty -
I'm with you always, to the glorious end."

18th April, 2010

Father Knows

He saw my tears
He saw my fears
He saw me cringe
From unknown terrors
He saw me wandering
In the wilderness
Not knowing what I was doing
Not knowing how I got there.

Yet He knew me
Before I was born, drew me
Called me His own
Hid me in His refuge
Covered my sins
Blotted out my shame
Cleansed me, dressed me
In His robe of righteousness.

Thoughts of God

Somewhere in the recesses
Of my mind, I knew
That Father knows
That Father won't forget me
That Father won't leave me
Somewhere deep down
Though covered by thick dark clouds
I knew, that Father knows.

Father kept calling
Calling me home
Calling me back
"You are Mine
I have redeemed you
Return to me daughter
I'm here to get you
Just take My hand."

I couldn't get it
I strained to hear His voice
Sweet and still
Prompting me to Himself
I thought I was truly lost
I felt Father was gone
That He didn't want me
Didn't love me anymore.

The more I cringed
The more He reached out
The louder the voices got
The more He spoke His Word
Because Father knew

That I never wanted to leave
I just did not know
How deadly the trap laid for me.

But Father, O Father
All knowing, all-seeing Father
With deep pity and great love
Bowels of compassion
O love that would not let go
Got me, touched and raised me
All muddy, all messy, yet
He did that, because He knows.

He embraced me, kissed me
Welcomed me back home
Said, "There's still a long way to go
But I'll work until I see
That your mess becomes a message
And your test a testimony
I'll work until I see you
Conformed to the image of My Son."

So here I am, Father
Back where I truly belong
Longing for You to hold me
So safe and close in Your arms
Never let me go, Daddy
Because I truly love You so
It's just so beautiful to know
Father cares, Father knows.

11th April, 2010

Reflections Nine — April 15, 2008

Eternal God

I wrote this *Reflection* on my 43rd birthday in 2008. This is what I wrote to my friends: "Rejoice with me, for God has done wonderful things for me. 43 years ago on 15th April, He decided to "interrupt" His work and usher me into this big, big, universe and place me on a tiny brownish spot called planet earth. With all the teeming numbers of human beings, the whirlwind of constant activities and movements across the globe, He remembered me. Infact before I was formed, He knew me. He saw my frame. He knew my name. He knew my times and my seasons and He targeted me for His salvation and the fulfillment of His purpose. And oh, how He has been totally mindful of me even when I didn't know Him! The Eternal God, who dwells in the eternity of eternities, whose name is Alpha and Omega, the Beginning and the End, who has no beginning or end, chose to create me, and have a relationship with me! He caused limited Time to pay attention to me, so that as insignificant as I am in this space called Earth, Time will continue to pay attention to me until God "interrupts" again, one day when He decides I join Him to share His eternal timelessness… the real thing. For now, at age 43 and counting, my business is to make sure I remember how short earth's Time is, when compared with the Eternal; how fleeting the earth's joys are, when compared with the promised eternal treats of heaven.

"When I consider Your heavens, the work of your fingers... what is man that You are mindful of him, and the son of man that You visit him? Psalm 8:2 (NKJV)

Yes, I pray to see at least a great, great, grandchild, but no earthly joy can compare with the day I see Jesus face to face. Just imagine!!!"

Eternal God, Eternal Arms

I may not understand -
But why should I blame God?
Through it all He's been with me
The eternal God is my refuge
And underneath, His everlasting arms. [35]

In sickness, in my pain
In perplexity, in distress
I haven't fallen through the cracks
The eternal God is my refuge
And underneath, His everlasting arms.

In many tears, through many wakes
In pangs of fears, in a stormy mind
I haven't caved in, I'm not destroyed
The eternal God is my refuge
And underneath, His everlasting arms.

Why should I complain?
Though I can ask questions
He still calls me, to reason together
The eternal God is my refuge
And underneath, His everlasting arms.

Yes Lord, I have questions
I wonder, I analyze, I ask, I ask
Yet I will not fall, I will not fail
The eternal God is my refuge
And underneath His everlasting arms.

And through it all
The end shall surely come
His Blood, His Name, His love will secure
The eternal God is my refuge
And underneath, His everlasting arms.

10th March, 2010

Without Spot or Wrinkle*

One day in eternity past,
The Son said to the Father,
"I am preparing, *Abba**
To take for Myself a bride."

"You know Father," continued the Son,
"How much You love the children of Adam;
Though they have strayed and sinned,
It's time to put The Plan into action."

"Son", said the Father,
"This is going to be hard,
Because My heart will break so much
To see what You'd go through."

"I wish there was some other way, Son,
But blood must be shed, the purest blood;
That alone can cleanse the depths of their sin;
That alone can break the great wall of separation."

"It would be so hard to see You suffer so;
Here in Heaven I too will suffer, share Your pain;
I will turn My face away, I cannot bear it;
But go You must, for You love them so."

"Father", said the Son, "I will go,
I will die, and I will reconcile;
I will enable them to live for You;
The Bride I deserve, without spot or wrinkle."

"It'll be worth it Son, because You know,
That though I can create many other races
I have given My heart to Adam's race;
I can't let them go, I can't see them die."

"I will be with You Son, through it all;
Together with the Holy Spirit We'll succeed;
Though We will not take them by force,
If they love Us back, that'll be enough."

The angels cried to see Him go;
The Darling of Heaven, Bright Morning Star;

Joining humanity, mixing in its mess,
So to save, redeem and to bless.

So came the Son, He was named Jesus;
Born in a manger, acquainted with grief;
Man of many sorrows, rejected, despised;
Just so sinful man, undeserving, be redeemed.

He walked, He talked, He healed, He blessed;
He served, He taught, He loved, didn't condemn;
Persuaded even sworn enemies to see the truth,
Evident in scripture, evident in nature.

Rejected many times, He never gave up;
Went to the forsaken, the lame and the weak,
The sick, the marginalized, outside the wall,
Telling them the Gospel, the good news had come.

Then one day, Heaven stood still;
The time had come, the Son had to die;
There was no reprieve, purpose had to be fulfilled,
To bring back to Himself the Bride of Christ.

Gloom, doom, darkness and despair
All colluded and clapped in glee;
"We have Him where we want," they surmised,
"All His works have come to nought, humanity's done!"

Then came Sunday dawn, still dark;
The universe watched, Heaven stood attention;

Thoughts of God

Angels whispered to one another -
"Where's Holy Spirit? Where's He gone?"

They didn't know that the great battle was done;
The Son had descended, the Son had wrestled;
He disarmed the powers, made them a public spectacle;
Darkness fled, demons screeched, "alas, we're done."

For the Son had finished it with His dying breath;
He had ransomed His Bride, bought with a price;
In hell was one quest – the keys of Death and Hades -
That too He took, wrested from the prince of darkness.

Then with a shout, He rose from the grave;
Death could not hold Him, the grave had no power;
The Holy Spirit was on a mission, nothing could stop Him;
Christ is risen – the Son has won!

Heaven was in a frenzy of joy;
Nature stopped to worship in awe;
The Father on His Throne so proud, totally satisfied,
Said, "That's My Son, and We made it!"

One day in the not too distant future,
A great wedding will be performed;
A culmination of all the Father, Son and Spirit did,
For a Bride, without spot or wrinkle.

And I shall be there, not a mere guest,
But the Beloved, the purest Bride;
Prepared for a King, ransomed at great price,
The Prince of life Himself, my eternal Bridegroom!

*(*Title of Poem is taken from St. Paul's Letter to the Ephesians, Chapter 5:27. Written during a wedding ceremony I attended in Accra. ***Abba** is Aramaic for 'Father', better still, 'Daddy'!)*
11th April, 2010

Reflections Ten   April 22, 2008

The Power of God

Yes, our God is so powerful. Creator, King, God. He works wonders with His mighty right hand and outstretched arm. He is a consuming fire. Infact, no one or nothing can withstand His presence. He is awesome indeed. But is it not simply amazing to discover that God chooses not to use His absolutely superior might to get us to relate to Him? God hardly comes to us in a big bang, frightening us into submission; He does not control, override or push His way through to bend us to His will. Infact God uses the most surprising ways to come into our hearts; to get our attention concerning what He is doing in our world: He comes through a fugitive (Moses), [36] a shepherd boy (David), [37] a talking donkey (who belonged to the prophet Balaam), [38] a childless woman (Hannah), [39] a nondescript virgin girl (Mary), [40] a widow (with two copper coins), [41] a half-gentile woman with questionable sexual lifestyle credentials (the woman of Samaria), [42] a child (whom Jesus took in His arms and blessed), [43] a despised tax-collector (Zacchaeus), [44] the poor (to whom the kingdom belong), [45] a manger (at Bethlehem), [46] and most shocking, a cross (at Calvary or Golgotha).[47] There are countless other examples strewn across the Bible. His greatest act of power towards us- to snatch us from the jaws of eternal death and separation from His presence- was to come all the way down and be nailed to a wooden cross, the most accursed and despicable way of death for a criminal. This, the Bible says, is the foolishness of God; [48] foolish to those who refuse to understand how a so-called all powerful God can act that way, but to us, this is the real thing – the cross is the power of God! [49]

"But God has chosen the foolish things of the world to put to shame the wise, and God has chosen the weak things of the world to put to shame the things which are mighty." I Corinthians 1:27 (NKJV)

I need to remind myself of this daily, that I shouldn't be too impressed with myself and my so-called social or academic accolades; or about big armies, huge buildings, flashy cars; mega-ministries with body guards and other trappings. God may, after all, not be impressed at all…

He Ran*

I never noticed that phrase before;
Don't think I paid any attention to it.
Today it hit me as I did my devotion -
Father ran to meet the prodigal son!

God the Almighty, Sovereign, great?
He ran to meet His prodigal son.
It means He left His throne in the Temple
And stood at the gate, waiting for His son.

He must have been stretching His royal neck,
Looking out upon the horizon;
Longing for, waiting and waiting
For the black sheep, His prodigal son.

And what did He do, when He saw him,
Afar off and approaching timidly
With dusty feet, flat stomached, in dire need -
Father ran and caught Him to His breast!

"Welcome home son, I've longed for you;
Yes you did wrong, but I forgave;
Even before you left, I prepared for today -
Praying and willing you back again."

So has it been ever since,
That God our Father waits for us;
When we sin and when we run
He wants us back with Him again.

Indeed does He leave His all;
Run to meet us as we come;
Because He's been waiting all along
To put on us our royal robes.

What grace, what love, what mercy;
For the Alpha and Omega, Sovereign One
To do this for His wayward sons -
Thank You Lord, my "Running Highness"!

(*Based on the parable of the Prodigal Son in Luke Chapter 15: 11-32)
18th June, 2010

The Power of the Cross

O the power of the Cross!
O the depths of the Cross!
O the love upon the Cross!
Help me know, help me hold;
Help me wrap my mind around it;
My heart, my soul and my being.
Help me envision the depths
Christ would go to save me;
Help me never to hold it lightly,
That in knowing I would know,
That He did it for loves' sake;
Love for me, love that would not let go,
Still holds me, sound and secure.
Even when I strain and stray,
The power of the Cross reaches across;
The love of the Cross draws me back.
So Lord, I say today and say again,
That Your pain will ne'er be in vain;
I love You Lord, I love You too,
As foolish as I many times am;
Forgetting what lengths You'd go,
To give me new life and a new hope;
To translate me from darkness to light.
Forgive me, when my mind says things -
My heart is intact, my spirit is Yours;
Bring my mind under Your control,
Your Spirit's rule, Your loving care.
Let me be united to fear Your name;
To love You with body, soul and spirit.

The Cross is my victory, glory and hope -
O the power of the Cross!

(Written on a particularly challenging and distressing day… yet the love and the power of the Cross still broke through for me.)

Reflections Eleven   December 17, 2007

Where is Jesus?

If asked, "Where is Jesus?" most of us Christians would reply, "in my heart." Indeed, He is in our hearts, if we have asked Him to cleanse us of all our sins and come in to live with us. How do I know? I know because His Word says so, simple and short. But He also invites us to walk with Him, and participate in what He is doing, where He is. And where is that? In a sense, He is everywhere in His omnipresence; but specifically He is walking and working among the broken, the battered, the weak and wretched of the earth. He is still walking among those who know they have no sufficiency in themselves. Oh, we may build glorious temples and cathedrals for Him, and yes, He deserves the beauty we honor Him with; but He is not impressed if our hearts are not beautified, touched and transformed by His life. If He was impressed, the amazing cathedrals and worship edifices of Europe would not now be tourist sites, filled by a handful of worshippers. God is where He is working, and if I truly want to be with Him and work with Him to fulfill the one single desire of His heart - for humankind to know His deep, deep love and His salvation then I have to go with Him, otherwise He'll leave me in my comfortable, beautiful church house to pursue a religion of my own making and go looking for those whose hearts are crying out for His salvation and His true comfort.

My compassionate Jesus, who walks among the weary and scattered, sheep without a shepherd; who feels what they feel, so He can truly be the Shepherd of their souls.

"...So He became their Savior. In all their affliction He was afflicted, and the Angel of His Presence saved them; In His love and His pity He redeemed them; And He bore them and carried them, all the days of old." Isaiah 69: 8b-9 (NKJV)

Are we looking for Jesus? He still walks among the poor, the battered and the weak, to pick them up and bring them to green pastures and quiet waters. Let us go with Him.

Jesus of The Catacombs*

He knew a storm was brewing over the lake;
Yet He set the unknowing disciples to sail;
He knew someone important was waiting,
On the other side for His intervention.

So in obedience the disciples set to sail;
With their Master, across the lake;
Calm and peaceful it all seemed,
But suddenly the winds came blowing in.

They tried to row, to steer, to keep
The boat afloat to avoid the deep;
Tried all they could, nothing could be,
Sinking fast, the waters splashing in.

Hearts pounding, in panic they cried:
"Alas Master", they rushed to His side,
"Do You not care that we perish?"
They couldn't see then, that was not His wish.

For He had said, "Let us go to the other side"-
Knowing definitely that His word would abide;
Nothing was going to stop His purpose;
Neither nature, nor demon His will could douse.

"Why are you so afraid, little ones?
Do you not know the One who comes
With the Spirit of the Lord, anointed,
To save, set free, at the time appointed?"

"Be still," He said, and all at once,
The waves fled, calmed their crazy dance;
A lesson to His disciples in faith and recognition,
As they watched in awe the Master on a mission.

Now all safely on the other side,
Someone unknowingly did abide;
Deep in the catacombs, tombs of darkness;
An outcast, stronger than any chain or harness.

Feared, avoided, lost in oppression,
Didn't even have the faculty to reason;

Inhabited by a thousand demons,
In total darkness; but one day, light dawns.

For this one's sake the storm had arisen
To stop the Savior on His mission;
But this is Jehovah, Redeemer, Friend,
Walking in the catacombs, a captivity to end.

At first sighting the mad man cried:
"What have You to do with us at this side?"
This was not the man the Creator made,
This one besieged, a captive, a slave.

But it is written: "Even the lawful captive
Will be taken away," and thereby live;
And "the prey of the terrible be delivered"[50] -
The promise stands; but this one too, a beloved?

One so totally gone, a living dead;
Walked in the catacombs, there made his bed;
No inkling of faith to so deserve
The attention of the Master, no such nerve.

But this Holy God, so completely love,
Sent Jesus, God in flesh from above;
For people such as one formerly called 'Legion',
The mad, mad man of the Gadarene.

The Lord went to him, sought him out;
The foreign invaders, no chance, came out;
Screeching, fleeing; redemption dawned,
On one totally lost, without hope and pawned.

Thoughts of God

Jesus, Savior, walked the catacomb,
His helplessly lost sheep to draw back home;
His kingdom reaches into the darkest places;
He knows every situation, all shades and faces.

It doesn't matter how deep the captivity;
How far lost, gone, the aggression or passivity;
It doesn't matter the source or reason -
Spiritual, social, mental – there is a season.

He comes to the catacombs, among the tombs;
Obsessives, 'schizos', whatever the dooms;
Psychos, paranoids, autistics and epileptics;
The abused, broken, battered He picks.

Inside all of them, of us, a light dawns;
Created for His glory, not mere pawns;
He still comes through, still communicates
His undying love, wretched souls He saves.

Yes, something went wrong, not always explained;
Dark clouds, dark thoughts, a mind maimed;
Sin, self, nature, enemy attack or circumstances,
Work alone or collude to rig the captive's chances.

But God not partial, not discriminating,
Lights His light in dark nights, alternating;
Bringing His truth to counter lies and deception;
Breaking barriers and boundaries in redemption.

Do I have hope for that autistic child,
Who seems barely to feel an emotion mild?

Or for the epileptic, passing out, falling into fire,
Many in straits so sad, so bad, so dire?

Do I have hope for that broken-hearted woman,
Victim of infidelity, abuse, a life all but done?
Or for that one who curses uncontrollably,
Crying for help, lost in hopeless captivity?

Do I have hope for one who hears voices,
Other than his own, a mind of din and noises,
Or that one who repeatedly self- harms,
Urged by seemingly invisible hands?

Jesus who walks the catacombs,
Searching not only in temple domes,
Even for those whose minds seemed walled
Like the walls around Jericho, still He called.

Called to come to the Savior's love,
Who gives beauty for ashes, peace like a dove;
Breaks through with commanding force,
To rescue His own; open iron-clad doors.

Jesus, Lord over the catacombs,
In Him alone dwell all the hopes
Of those who can sometimes barely see,
That glimmer of light, that freedom key.

To unlock the secret gates of captivity;
To draw out the prisoners of Gadarene;
To bring to a place of quiet, calm and peace;
To give the once misunderstood a life lease.

That brings joy and everlasting life,
A place of sunshine and of light;
Never again to wander, wonder or fear,
Only close to our caring Savior so dear.

Yes, there is a season, a definite time,
When Jesus will visit, even touch the slime;
Though it tarries, it surely, certainly comes,
My Jesus, definitely Lord over the catacombs.

(*Based on the Biblical accounts of Jesus' encounter with the man formerly called Legion, in Matthew Chapter 8, Luke Chapter 8 and Mark Chapter 4)
3rd August, 2010

You've Been There

Once tired, You have become our rest;
Once hungry, You have become our bread;
Once sweating, You have become our shade;
Once bleeding, You have become our healer.

Once forsaken, You have made us accepted;
Once rejected, You have made us beloved;
Once weeping, You have become our joy;
Once deformed, You have made us beautiful.

Once thirsty, You are our living waters;
Once walking, You are our way of life;
Once grieving, You have filled us with laughter;
Once dying, You are our Resurrection.

Thoughts of God

Once humbled, You are our King of Kings;
Once serving, You show us the way;
Once nailed, You are our Redeemer;
Once broken, You are our restorer.

Once in the flesh, You became our immortality;
Once in darkness, You became the light of the world;
Once in the grave, You gave us the passport to heaven;
Once risen, You conquered the world!

20th July, 2010

Reflections Twelve   February 18, 2008

Sanctuary and Solitude

Sanctuary and Solitude are two sisters. Sanctuary - a place of *hiddeness*; of covering, of safety. Aaah... How I love to run into that place! And oh what peace I often forfeit when I forget to run there! Sanctuary is a high tower with the Name of the Lord written on her wall, and the Bible says "the righteous run into it and are safe."[51] And then there is Solitude - a place of Aloneness, not loneliness, or lonesomeness, but Aloneness. Alone, but with One who fills all and never leaves me lonely - Christ my God. In the noise and din of this rushing world, I am learning to go into the Sanctuary to look for Solitude. I am learning that it is possible to be in a room filled with a thousand people and still seek Sanctuary and Solitude whose arms are forever wide open to be what I know them to be - a covering and a silent communion - by God and with God. A.W Tozer talks about the "Inward Gaze",[52] a period when one goes "inside" to connect momentarily with the Most High in any or all circumstances. That is what Sanctuary and Solitude do for me, transporting me to gentle green pastures and still waters; with my Shepherd standing close by with His staff in His hand, lovingly watching me graze. A covering, and a rest.

'Says the Lord God, the Holy One of Israel: "In returning and rest you shall be saved; In quietness and confidence shall be your strength." Isaiah 30:15 (NKJV)

Have I painted the picture for you? Stop for a moment. Sanctuary and Solitude are silently beckoning...

Only so far

In the shelter of Your loving arms
In the covering of Your mighty hand
In the hedge of Your protection
In the hiddenness of Your love -
There's only so far
That the enemy can go.

I may not fully grasp why
I go through all I go through
I know one thing, sure of it too
That my Anchor holds through the storm -
There's only so far
That the enemy can go.

God's promises remain forever true
Come hell or high-water, fire or desert storm
He never leaves, never forsakes
The broken hedge only appears so -
There's only so far
That the enemy can go.

For the Lord has set a standard
He has lifted the bar, the plumb line
The Holy Spirit watches over to perform

As I hide in the shadow of His wings -
There's only so far
That the enemy can go.

Thus will I hide, thus will I cling
Never let You go no matter how hard
But I am weak and You are strong
So You'll hold me, firm and long -
There's only so far
That the enemy can go.

10th March, 2010

The Child

In simple trust
And childlike faith
Let me be this child
Who loves You, simply.

Like a weaned child
On the breast of Mother
So let me be this child
Who hears You, simply.

Like a child at rest
With little care in a storm
Let me be this child
Who trusts You, simply.

When life brings surprises
Inexplicable pain or sorrow
Let me be this child
Who knows Your name, simply.

You are Abba, my Father
You really do love me
Let me be this child
Who embraces You, simply.

9th April, 2010

Reflections Thirteen   April 30, 2008

Submission and Surrender...

Submission and Surrender are twin brothers. Infact, they are so alike it's uncanny. They go everywhere together and do things together - they might as well have been Siamese twins. The sad thing is, no one likes Sub and Sur (their aliases) much, not even Christians. Anytime I encounter these two, they solemnly look at me and stare me straight in the eyes with their silent questions. Sub says to me, "Is Jesus your Savior, truly your Lord?" And Sur says, "Angela, have you truly given up everything you have, know and do for Jesus?" Hey, these two are not the easiest of fellows to deal with, my friends, because what they are asking me to do is not even a one day, one time thing, done once and for all; it's a daily demand to die to myself! And I tell you, as a human rights advocate who 'fights,' as it were, against injustices to women and children, sometimes I'm not sure anymore. So I say to Sub and Sur, "I don't know all of what I've left to myself today, but whatever they are, whoever they are, I drag them out of me, dead or alive, and give to Jesus. Work on it for me Lord, because You are the One who is able to perfect that which concerns me, You the Author and *Perfecter* of my faith. Work on it." Somehow, Sub and Sur smile at me, as though somewhat content with my answer. They turn and with their big, solemn eyes, bid goodbye to me and say, "See you tomorrow, Angela." Hmm...

"If anyone desires to come after Me, let him deny himself, and take up his cross daily, and follow Me."
Luke 9:23

It's another day my friends. It's another day.

Take It All

Lord I can't hold on with my willpower;
I can only determine to hold on
To Your garments; to the faith
You have clothed me with.

For it is only by grace that I am saved,
By faith in the Son of God
Who loved me, and gave Himself for me;
And I believe this with all my heart.

I know Christ alone is my Savior, my plea;
But why does there come a time
When it feels as though I must hang on
With all of my mind's faculties?

I know that by strength no one shall prevail; [53]
It's not by power, nor might, but by Your Spirit; [54]
So dear Lord Jesus, all I can say is this:
Hear me Lord, please hear my heart –

Thoughts of God

You know me, my intentions and imaginations;
You know me better than I know myself;
You are my Judge; You also are my Advocate;
In Your loving hands I know I'm safe.

To You I leave my will and determination -
Determined to love You, help me to love You;
Determined to serve You, help me serve You;
Determined to follow You, help me follow You.

You are my life, my "exceedingly great reward". [55]
You make me, or I am not made;
You mold me, or I cannot stand;
You prune me, or I cannot grow;

Simply, I am Yours, I can't be anything else;
Were I not, You would not stick by me -
Through thick and thin, faith and faithlessness;
You have remained constant, true and faithful.

Knowing me better than I know myself,
I beseech You to show me my heart;
I beseech You to transform my being
Into the image of my Savior, Your Son.

I trust You Lord, to let me die
To self, so I can truly live to You;
To sin, so I can truly be divine;
To the world, so I can taste of heaven.

I need You so deeply for my soul;
I need Your light and to be my delight;

Help me Lord, I beseech You,
The cry of my heart, to be truly Yours.

Amen.
Father's Response:
You are Mine, daughter, says the Lord;
Do not beat up on yourself so.
Yes, I know you better than you know yourself,
I've known you through eternity;
I called you, chose you to be Mine.
The adversary has assailed your defenses, I know,
He touched your mind with his arsenal of lies.
But do not be afraid, I am with you;
Have always been, will always be.
I will fight for you, I will deliver and save - [56]
I've told you many times, so now please listen:
Don't miss the sun because of the clouds;
Don't miss the tree because of the forest;
I am with you, and for always.
I live to work in you, both to will,
And for My own good pleasure. [57]
I am not fickle, arbitrary or capricious;
I know the plans I have for you; [58]
Never to destroy you, but to set you right;
To set you straight and to make you Mine;
More and more to become like My Son. [59]
Rest in Me, Daughter, just rest in Me;
Stop struggling and fretting, still your heart;
Trust me, daughter; you'll turn out fine you'll see.
I'll cause You to know Me more, you desire it so;
I'll heal your backslidings, heal your wounds; [60]
And I'll write My law upon your heart. [61]

I'll cause My countenance to shine upon you; [62]
Do not be afraid, only believe, and hold on.
I hear your every prayer, know your heart;
And yes, I'll cause your faith to grow,
Even as you reach out with the little and exercise. [63]
So will you see Me, know Me and grow
Taller as each day's challenges and storms pass,
And you see victory upon victory, enemies fall;
You will know without a shadow of doubt,
That I'm with you always, and eternally.

Still Yours,

Father.

20th July, 2010

A Life to Live

It is more than enough to be saved,
The greatest gift of all – God's love,
Demonstrated beyond all reasonable doubt -
God on the Cross!

But there's this life to live,
A life dedicated, committed to Him,
Who died that we might live:
A walk on the straight and narrow.

It's the road that leads us
To the pearly gates of Heaven;

It's strewn with mountains and dangers;
With wolves in sheep's clothing.

There are tears, moans and groans;
But there are joys plentiful,
For the Master of this road
Walks beside and ahead of us.

He says to us, "I am the Light;
Follow Me and the dark clouds,
Though ever present can never overtake,
Because I am here to keep My own."

So Lord I pray so fervently,
Thanking You for my great salvation;
Knowing that You will surely lead me
To God - on the Throne.

To remember all that He did
To take all my sins away,
May I constantly focus on You, Lord,
While we walk this road to Heaven.
Amen!

Reflections Fourteen   October 6, 2007

It's not about me....

Sometimes I ask myself, and Jesus, 'Lord, am I truly surrendered to You?' Then I tell myself and I tell Him, 'Lord, you know me better than I know myself. You know my heart; you know those parts of me that are truly surrendered, and those that I am keeping back. I want to be totally surrendered. Take it all - my head, my nose, my eyes, my heart, my legs, my dreams, my knowledge, my human rights, my evangelical feminism, my children, my husband, my relationships... everything! Lord, everything...'

"The wind blows wherever it pleases. You hear its sound, but you cannot tell where it comes from or where it is going. So it is with everyone born of the Spirit." John 3:8

Because, you know what? It's no longer about me. He knew me in eternity past, and knows my eternity future. He knows and understands all my blind spots, and those parts of my heart that are hidden from my own view. King David was that kind of man who knew too well that sometimes children of God make mistakes they never meant to commit, and presume certain things which end up on the wrong side of God, without meaning to. Thus David cried in Psalm 19 v. 12: "Who can understand his errors? Cleanse me from secret faults…" Thank God for being a Father who is mindful of the frailty and foolishness of His children, and although He does not excuse sin, makes every provision for total forgiveness, as we truthfully surrender to Him all our known and 'unknown' parts, with all our heart. Father knows where I've come from, and where I'm going... He fixes me up and charts my paths-and so I can say with confidence: it is well with me. Isn't that just great?

Thank You Daddy

It's hard for me to express
How I feel, what I want to say,
But I know You know exactly what it is.
Words fail me, but the Spirit knows,
For He searches my heart.
Sometimes I really wonder
Why You care about me so much;
I don't think I'm all that special
And there are billions of others.
But now I know without a doubt
That You made the decision
To choose me, and to love me
Inspite of myself and all You know
And imputed Your righteousness to me
As if I'd never sinned before...

Knowing this keeps me going
When darkness covers and trials assail;
When temptation incites to give up -

I learn to give in to Your love
Which covers all, then I go on.
Thank You, Daddy, Father mine,
Who has made me truly Thine;
There's nothing I can ever add
To so great a work of salvation;
Not one deed, not a word.
Thus while in this world I strive
To do my Father's perfect will,
I know He'll strengthen me by day
To get me to His holy hill.

All praise, all glory, all honor to You,
My King faithful, my Shepherd and all;
Who has kept me close to Your breast,
In all circumstances and places,
Through the changing seasons.
To You I owe my everything -

Words fail me, Lord...
This is how much I can say.

1st June, 2010 at Mitcham, Surrey, London

Conquering By the Cross

Followers of Christ,
Conquer by the cross;
They sow in tears,
They reap in joy.

They bear their cross,
Lightened by Christ;
They cry many tears,
Everlasting joy is theirs.

They mourn for the world
And work to save many;
With Christ by their side,
Enabled to conquer.

Take up your cross
And follow the Christ;
The burden of discipleship,
Is the crown of *followership*.

But this yoke is easy
And His burden is good; [64]
Because He's always there
To bear it with us.

He provides the light,
On the dark patches;
He bears us in His arms
When weariness surpasses.

True followers of Christ,
Will take up their cross;
And faithfully follow
Till they be conquerors.

Crosses are for conquerors;
Obstacles for overcomers;

Battles for kings
And sacrifice for priests.

All these and more,
Are what Christ has called us for;
Conquerors by the Cross
Will suffer earthly loss.

There's certainly a cost,
To following the Christ;
But oh, how worthwhile,
To get to the glorious Prize!

21st June, 2010

Reflections Fifteen   October 27, 2007

Move that mountain!!!

There were times in my life, when as a young(er) woman, I would remember the words of Jesus in Matthew 17 v. 20, "If you have faith as a mustard seed, you will say to this mountain 'move from here to there,' and it will move..." Silly me, I would fix my eyes on a hill close to my neighborhood, then close them tightly to muster big faith and say "Move!" Of course, they never went anywhere...Why? Because God did not mean for me to treat faith as a magic wand, conjuring up images of my own prowess. Could God have literally moved those hills? Yes. Remember He stopped the sun? [65] But He wants me to understand deeply, that *He has all power, all wisdom, and He is all good!* My faith is to know that He is bigger than ANYTHING I can possibly imagine or encounter, and He is able, and willing to change my difficult circumstances. My part is to know Him and trust Him and ask Him, ask Him, ask Him, and also trust Him, trust Him, trust Him. The combination of His power, wisdom and goodness towards me is what will bring the answer that fits His will for my life-perfectly! Could God have stopped the incarnate Jesus, Son of God, going to the cross? Absolutely. But did He when Jesus asked? No, because Jesus' desire to be spared the alienation of the cross was submitted to God's perfect will and purpose, which was the way of the cross. Because of this exercise of God's perfect will, that "impossible" mountain of humankind's separation from God was moved! To a nearly 100 year-old childless man God said:

"Look now toward heaven, and count the stars... so shall your descendants be." Genesis 15: 5

Impossible! But the Bible tells us:

"And he (Abram) believed the Lord, and He accounted it to him for righteousness." Genesis 15: 6

Even I, am a descendant of Abraham, included some four or more thousand years ago in God's promise to the man. Imagine that! In any dire situation, God is able, and He is willing! He is my exceedingly great reward and He, and His perfect will, should be the sole object of my faith. Let us trust Him!

The Focus

The storms will come;
The dangers will arise;
The enemy will assemble;
What matters is the focus.

Whoever said,
The Christian life is cheesecake -
All sweet, no troubles,
All joy, no sorrows?

Thoughts of God

Whoever said,
Faith tested is easy,
Battles won't bring bruises,
Discouragement won't come?

Whoever said,
God's heroes here are perfect,
Without blemish and stains,
Without spots and wrinkles?

Whoever said,
Righteousness, peace,
Joy in the Holy Ghost,
Is a state reached at once?

The truth is there
For all to see;
The Master trod the road
And so shall we.

Dusty feet, tiredness,
Groanings within;
Persecutions, distresses,
And even tears.

But in all these things,
Great conquerors are we,
If we focus on the One
Who trod the path and won.

He did not bear our pain,
So we don't go through pain;

He bore the Cross,
So we can bear ours too.

He took away our shame,
So when shame comes,
We look up to the One
Who brings us radiance.

He took our infirmities
And bore our diseases, [66]
To show us that in Him
We have a wounded Healer.

He went from city to town;
From synagogues to Temple;
We too will travel a road
Both of rocks and of beauty.

But whoever said,
That joy will be small?
It will so bubble,
That it'll be inexpressible

Whoever said,
Peace will be elusive?
It will be so abundant
That we can share with others.

Whoever said,
That grace's supply is short?
Grace will add to grace,
Greater than all our sin.

Whoever said,
Faith will wane and finish?
He who promised is faithful,
And also able to keep.

Whoever said,
Love will ever be lacking?
The One who called us
Is Himself love.

Goodness and mercy will follow; [67]
Truth and justice in tow;
Righteousness will clothe,
So we'll always follow.

All the pain and sorrows,
All the rocks and furrows,
Whatever the cost
All is worth the prize.

For Christ is the focus
And Christ is the prize;
Christ in us, Christ with us,
Christ in God, Christ in all.

19th April, 2010

Perseverance

Stay.

Though the mountains do not move
Though the situation changes not
Though you've prayed your heart out -
Stay.

Though you ask and ask
And all seems quiet
Though the story seems like a life sentence -
Stay.

Though it feels like enemy territory
And all support is gone
Though you're in the sea for three days -
Stay.

Stay at the feet of Jesus
He never fails to come through
In every great story
Told of the saints of heaven
Trial and perseverance
Are as sure as the morning sun
Rising on the horizon
There is a call to wait
There is a test to stay.

One day soon before you know
The mountains will certainly move -
God will surprise you as He's wont to do

So hold on friend, just stand still
And see the salvation of the Lord.
Stay.

6th June, 2010

Reflection Sixteen   September 22, 2007

We don't have all the answers...

Indeed this life can be a big puzzle, and we don't have all the answers to all of life's great questions; but we still trust in the One who has all the answers, and holds us, and the whole world in His perfect hands. There's a line in a song I love to hear, and it goes: "Who imagined the sun and gave source to its light, yet conceals it to bring us the coolness of night...?"* Indeed, who did? I know my Father did, but *how* did He imagine it? Thus when I don't quite understand *how come* a great believer loses all his children in one incident, and life still goes on inspite of great pain and grief, I can only give one response – Lord You know it all. I may not understand fully, but I will learn to trust you. Lord, You know why, how, how come, what is, and what will be, and truly we are grieving and we are hurting, but we will trust!

"I will meditate also of all your work, and talk of your doings. Thy way O God, is in the sanctuary; who is so great a God as our God? You are the God who does wonders; You have declared your strength among the people." **Psalm 77:12-14**

As I ponder the mysteries of life and how little I know of anything, I rest in the One who has all knowledge, wisdom and power. I invite you to rest in Him too!

(*A line in a song by Chris Tomlin titled "Indescribable",
©Six Step Records, 2004

The Wonder of It All

In Your justice there is great mercy;
In Your great power lies amazing love
What sort of a God are You?
Show me Your great gentleness.

For You see my heart now, Lord.
I don't feel lost anymore... just sad,
Because I heard a dear one
Has just passed on.

I am not confused anymore,
But my brow is furrowed
Is life all futile, Lord?

No, it's not, because You are *the* life;
The real life, here and hereafter.
And Lord You indeed are my life,
And the whole length of my days.
I would have it no other way, Jesus

I am lost without You,
Nothing without You -
That is how I feel Lord, now.

Sometimes my heart feels
Like it is closed up,
But You open it gently, until
I feel Your love lift me up again-
Your gentle power and fierce love.
The wonder of it all –
For me, alive and in the hereafter…

Keep my friend hidden in You, eternally.

(Written during the final funeral rites of a good friend. He was forty and much loved by family, friends and work colleagues).
25th February, 2010

Why? Or Why?

It is not why me, Lord,
It is why did it happen?
What is the lesson?
What must I know?
How can it change me?
How can it prune me?
How can it mold me?

Am I learning?
Yes, everyday -
Of battle and empathy;
Of survival and grace;
Of courage and support;
Of the power of prayer and love:
Of a God who just won't let me go.

Thoughts of God

Trial, test, temptation or proving,
I may not know exactly what,
But one thing that I know -
God has been with me through it all;
Every day, every new challenge,
He's walked with me, dried my tears;
Enabled me on, through water and fire.

25th February, 2010

Reflections Seventeen September 30, 2007

His compassions fail not...

"Your steadfast love extends to the heavens... Your faithfulness, reaches to the clouds, Your righteousness is like majestic mountains, and Your wisdom like the depths of the sea... and You come to me...", says a not so contemporary Christian song.* Just thinking through it and saying to myself, if my own goodness were dependent on me, then I'm a total goner! It amazes me that His perfect love is so able to cast out the fear that somehow I can never measure up- because truly, I can't. It is the Blood of Jesus that is my only plea for righteousness and goodness…

"I say to the Lord, You are my Lord. Apart from You I have no good thing." Psalm 16:2 (NKJV)

Don't you just agree with David?

(*A song by Ted Sandquist; performed by Don Moen, © Lion of Judah Music, 1974)

In Your Blood

Covered by Your robe of righteousness
By Your sacrifice on Calvary's Cross;

In Your Blood are the hues of my life -
Rich colors of the different shades of my being.

Blessed am I indeed, because
You've imputed to me Your righteousness;
In Your Blood is woven the seasons of my life -
Dry, wet; winter, spring, summer and fall.

Each season's shade is as important as the other;
The dark hues mold my character;
The lighter hues are Your smiles upon my brow -
My coat of many colors – In Your Blood!

(At Evensong, St. Paul's Cathedral, London)
28*th* May, 2010

Hesed*

I don't love you in half measures, daughter,
I have loved you with an everlasting love;
Its length begins in eternity
And ends in eternity.

It's a love beyond your imagination;
It brought the Almighty to His knees;
Submitting to death and ignominy,
So I could win you over.

In My love is everything you'd ever need;
My grace, kindness, protection and mercy;

My healing, refreshment and health,
My everything for you.

I don't stop loving you because you sin;
My love works to woo you back in;
My love reaches across every divide,
Imagined, real or otherwise.

If I had to die again I would,
But I don't have to – My death has finished it all;
In My death is your life;
In My wounds are your healing.

I don't love you in half measures, My love;
Know this truth and let it set you free.
I love you so completely;
I love you unconditionally.

My gentleness will make you great; [68]
My rebuke will make you strong.
The thorny road will draw you close,
My love encompasses all your experience.

I don't love you in half measures, daughter,
You are beloved, you are *Jeshurun*;* [69]
You are endearment in My heart,
And a special star in My realm.

(***Hesed** in Hebrew encompasses the lovingkindness of God.
*Jeshurun is a Hebrew term of endearment used by God to describe His people Israel)
6th June, 2010

Reflections Eighteen   October 13, 2007

"Fear not?"

Who says I do not fear? Many things-high rises, rats, dogs standing in my way on the neighborhood roads, airplanes taking off, especially when I'm in them- name them. Oh, at first I would say - "I'm not afraid, I'm not afraid..." while all the while I am an "afraidwoman"... But know what? I found there's no use pretending. Because I learnt that God does not come to take away my fear. He urges me to confront and tell Mr. Fear that there is Someone more powerful and more 'dangerous' than he is; Someone who says, and urges me to say, "The Lord is my light and my salvation, whom shall I fear?"(Psalm 27 v. 1) and, "The Lord is (my) keeper and (my) shade at my right hand...He will preserve (my) going out and (my) coming in..." (Psalm 121 v. 5, 8) and "But the very hairs of (my) head are all numbered..." (Luke 12 v. 7) Hey, as I say these words, and I say them again and again, and my mind captures the essence of the Word, and my heart registers its truth... I see Mr. Fear in the corner of my eye begin to take to his dirty heels, running faster than Marion Jones on steroids. [70] And then..."*OYA*"!*

"Are not two sparrows sold for a copper coin? And not one of them falls to the ground apart from your Father's will...Do not fear therefore; you are of more value than many sparrows." Matthew 10: 29, 31 (NKJV)

I tell you truly, I refuse to be oppressed. *"His eye is on the sparrow, and I know He watches over me..."** Isn't that just awesome?

(**"Oya"* is an expression commonly used in Ghana to indicate someone running away in panic. *A line in a song originally written by Civilla D. Martin and Charles H. Gabriel in 1905)

Don't Run Away, Daughter

It's okay to cry, It's okay not to be okay,
It's okay to say you are angry with Me;
It's okay to tell me you are afraid,
You are not sure about tomorrow,
You don't know what to do,
Or what to say when you are here.
It's ok to say you don't understand;
Just don't run away, daughter, stay.

I understand you perfectly;
I know you by name; I know your frame;
Remember that I sent My Son;
To feel what you feel, weep as you weep,
Know your pain, go through your grief;
Laugh with you, dine with you,
Share your joys, afflictions and sorrows;
All so He'll save you.

I tell you not to be afraid;
I say so because I have the answer

To all your fears and disquiet;
So when you are afraid, come.
When you are in pain, come.
When you're uncertain, come.
Don't run away, daughter, trust Me,
To listen, to know and to heal.

It hurts Me to see you run;
Try to hide what you truly feel.
Bare your heart to Me, Your God;
I'm here to help you through
And to help you overcome.
My Son went through it too –
Though never uncertain of My love,
He knew darkness, rejection and sorrow,
But He always held on to Me.

"Father, why have You forsaken Me?" [71]
I was with Him in His pain,
Though separated, His loss was your gain.
Now seated with Me high above
We watch over you to draw you out
Into the circle of our love.
Come and hear words of gentleness,
Of transforming grace and lovingkindness.
Don't ever run again, daughter Mine,
I love you more than you'd ever find.

Come to Me, daughter Mine;
I'll give you laughter, deep divine;
I'll give you fresh rain, and the smell of roses;
I will restore you to your rest;

And take away your loneliness.
I'll give you strength to walk again.
No empty promises, all of the above,
I've sworn by Myself to do this in love.

Come daughter, rest and be patient;
I'm working change and transformation;
Painful though it sometimes seems,
I'll never ride rough over your dreams;
Dreams of a bright tomorrow, a life with Me;
They'll come true My daughter, you'll see.
Run into your Father's arms and stay-
Never to run out- never, ever again.

17th July, 2010

Out Of The Ashes

Out of the ashes I rise
From despair, hopelessness, *lostness*...

But God!
Said He will never leave me
Never forsake me
Never let me go.

Out of the ashes I rise
To new life
Breath of freshness
To hope, faith and love.

In God!
Out of the ashes I rise
Again to dream
Of endless possibilities
Work towards fulfillment
Strengthen community.

In Christ!
Out of the ashes I rise –
By the Spirit I rise!

16th July 2008

Reflections Nineteen   January 28, 2008

Lion of the Tribe of Judah!

Hear Him ROOAAAR! The Lion of the Tribe of Judah! [72] Lion. The king of the forest; the king of beasts. But this Lion – He is the King of the Universe. The planets are His. The stars are His. He calls each of them by name. He gathers the waters of the earth in the palm of His hand. The cattle on a thousand hills are His. [73] Add up the majesty and power of all the kings and queens of the ancient world and multiply that with all the power of the presidents and prime ministers of the modern world; altogether they don't come up to His little toenail (or little claw?). When He is on the prowl the earth shakes and trembles; smoke comes up from His nostrils; devouring fire from His mouth. Darkness is under His feet. His roar is like thunder. He sends out His arrows and vanquishes the enemy. [74] This Lion, His eyes are everywhere, all at once! [75] Indescribable. Untamable. Simply Uncontainable. And just try to touch His anointed little ones…the little lions and lionesses, being you and I, [76] who have put our trust in Him! Blessed, happy, to be envied indeed, are those to whom the Lord does not impute iniquity; [77] those who have been washed by the Blood of King Lion, a.k.a "The Lamb of God" [78] (of all other names!!!).

"Behold, I have received a command to bless. He has blessed and I cannot reverse it. He has not observed iniquity in Jacob, nor has He seen wickedness in Israel.

The Lord his God is with him, AND THE SHOUT OF A KING IS AMONG THEM." Numbers 23:20b-21 (NKJV - Caps mine.)

Do you feel the elation I feel in my heart as I write this? There is nothing the enemy can do about me. Oh, he'll try, but he will not prevail. Aaah… how foolish I would be to wander away from my Father King Lion!

What is Your Shoe Size?

If Heaven is Your Throne
And earth is Your footstool [79]
What is the size of Your shoe?

The orb of the earth
And its teeming numbers
The hills, trees and rivers
The creatures and inventions
All things put together
Are not enough, Lord,
To make You a shoe.

You are the One
Who parts the sea with a mighty blow
Of wind from Your mouth.
You are the One who places Your foot
In the mighty, roaring waters;
Impossibilities are Your playthings;
Mountains of opposition are Your nothings.

Because You are so big, so strong
You are so mighty, so great;
There's nothing that You cannot do!
What seems so huge to me
Is but a dot, or a grasshopper to You.
If the whole earth is Your footstool,
Then what is the size of Your shoe?

Yet You came as one of humankind;
Such insignificant features we did not desire;
Born in a manger, raised in a village,
Took on my skin, limited to earth -
Just so You could save me.

Yet in my skin You were still King,
Sicknesses bowed, demons ran;
You crossed distances in nature
Without so much as a word;
In limited earthly flesh,
You brought heaven to earth.

You are glorious indeed,
Now risen seated far above again,
Above all principalities and all powers. [80]
Heaven is Your Throne,
The earth Your footstool;
Your shoe size is still unimaginable,
Wonder is, You've seated me with You!

So what's my shoe size now?
Big! The transformation is complete.
All things are made new!

But I'm learning to feel my way
To know my shoe size has truly changed;
Learning to walk upon my high hills,
Learning to trample down my arch enemy;
Learning to inspect my heav'n given possessions
Giving worship to the great I AM!

(Inspired by encouraging words from Shadrack, a Christian brother whom God placed in my way on a particularly challenging day in Accra)

17th July, 2010

Escapes from Death*

Unto the Lord indeed
Belong escapes from death! [81]

The Lord is mighty,
The Lord saves and will save;
He confounds the plans of the wicked;
He brings their counsel to nought.

Unto the Lord indeed
Belong escapes from death!

The Lord makes a way in the sea;
And highways in the wilderness;
He sends His armies to whip the enemy;
Fiercesome armies He brings to nought.

Unto the Lord indeed
Belong escapes from death!

He reveals to redeem,
He cuts the cords of the enemy;
He breaks the ploughs of the wicked in pieces;
He scatters the assembled with His hand.

Unto the Lord indeed
Belong escapes from death!

For whom does the Lord do this?
For He has nothing to lose in the least;
No one can raise a finger against Him;
But it is for me and for you His beloved.

Unto the Lord indeed
Belong escapes from death!

(*Inspired by Psalm 68 v. 20 and the miraculous escape of a wonderful Pastor, a great friend of my Mother's, from a gruesome death in an automobile accident in mid 2010)

Reflections Twenty   February 3, 2008

The Root of David...

"Before Abraham was, I AM", said Jesus in John 8 v. 58, in a discourse with Jewish authorities. He must have been a little over 30 years of age then. How shocked they must have been to see a young man, considered a rebel, an obnoxious renegade probably sporting long hair (if what the pictures depict are true), telling them He knows the Father; infact, that He *is* the Messiah sent by God; and to add insult to injury, if they did not believe Him, they were headed for the wrong side of eternity! The straw that broke the camel's back was when He boldly told them that He "IS BEFORE ABRAHAM"! What!!! That is where the Bible tells us that these dignified big men (did you hear of a female Pharisee? Don't question me, please) picked up stones to hurl at Him. It still did not occur to them when Jesus, to escape their wrath, "passed through the midst of them" without them noticing, that they were beholding in their time a phenomenon so great, a truth so deep, a Person so amazing- the One who dwells in eternity, who "begins" eternity, and "ends" eternity. Oh, if only they had opened their hearts a little; if only they had laid aside their own sense of importance as God's chosen ones; that "I am the IT" attitude that made them so short-sighted. They could not conceive that the Lord of eternity, who is 'before Abraham', who is the Root of David, would choose to make His home among mere mortals, starting His life among sheep and goats, dwelling in the little town of Nazareth, allowing 'spoiled' women to touch Him, suffering the most despicable insults and a most disgraceful death for his wayward, stiff-necked creatures. No, their kind of God would not do things like that. No way.

But my Bible says:

"And the WORD became flesh, and dwelt among us..."
John 1:14 (NKJV)

And:

"But He (Jesus), because He continues forever, has an unchangeable priesthood. Therefore He is also able to save to the uttermost those who come to God through Him, since He lives forever to make intercession for them." Hebrews 7:24-25 (NKJV)

Have you ever felt that you are in a place so filthy or so dark that God cannot reach down and pick you up? Or that you are too "big" to receive help? Then you haven't encountered the Root of David yet. He has felt it, lived it and seen it all - even before you and I were conceived. Let's go into the open arms of the sinless Lamb of God.

Before

You knew me, before;
You loved me, before;
You called me, before;
You saved me, before;
You delivered me, before.

You made me,
Before I was conceived;
You heard me cry out,
Before I ever lifted my voice;
You saw my distress,
Before my foot hit that stone;
You saw me sin,
Before I ever thought of Your grace.

You provided me grace,
Before I ever sinned;
You gave me a way of escape,
Before the temptation hit;
You laid out for me the way of the Cross,
Before I could ever conceive of heaven;
You prepared a bottle for my tears,
Before I ever cried out for mercy;

Light came,
Before I stepped into darkness;
Love lifted me,
Before I sank into the depths of despair;
Grace sustained me,
Before I saw myself as fallen.

In brokenness You received me,
Because Your Body had been broken for me, before;
In the bitterness of my cry You heard me,
Because You had been forsaken, before;
In the silence of the night You shone on me,
Because You were the light of the world, before.

Before I died, You made me alive;
Before I rose, You lifted me to the realms;
Before I was lifted, You seated me to reign with You;
Before I reigned with you, You made me like You;

O to fully know, understand, comprehend,
To apprehend what You accomplished, before.
In this is my hope, my rest and my glory,
My Christ - before.

(Written en route Kumasi to Accra, returning from a trip with my dear friend Janey)
27th February, 2010

Eternity's Time

I don't know what time it was in eternity,
When You descended into hell,
To wrest the keys of death from the Enemy,
And to preach to imprisoned spirits. [82]

For us it was three days and two nights,
According to this earth's timing,

But You are the Almighty, the Master of time,
A thousand years is but one day in Your sight.

As earth waited for the prophecy to come to pass,
Christ was at work having finished on the Cross,
He made assurance double sure for us,
Never again for the enemy to have the upper hand.

I believe there in the dark, dark grave,
Time stood still so Christ could accomplish,
His soul's deepest desire to save,
Earth's living souls and p'haps those long gone.

Our victory is done, our ransom paid,
It's ours to grasp, to hold and stay,
No matter what'er comes our way,
Our Lord is the Master of our life and destiny.

Reflections Twenty-one   January 20, 2008

I am Blessed...Everyday!

While studying at the University of Ghana in the mid eighties, I had a Professor of law who hated to hear people say "God's time is the best..." To him, that was a lazy man's excuse for non-performance. He used to say: "Every time is God's time!" Looking back, I now see the wisdom and truth of His words. Yes, in the fullness of time, God does exactly what He has planned to do before the foundation of the world, and His timing is *perfecto*! In essence, God's time for His planned purposes is always the best! But at the same time, He never ever stops working His good purposes in the lives of His children. When all seems quiet, He is still working, working, working, to perfect you and I who believe in Him and His Son Jesus. So I've learnt not to say "as for this year, I will be blessed." Infact, I get a bit surprised when people, especially believers say this as though God has a special year for blessing His children, because everywhere I turn I see the blessing of God on my life. It's everywhere. The little, the big, the medium, everywhere! I feel so blessed seeing this tiny little thing I had some umpteen years ago, grown into this big someone who now says to me "Mummy, but why? It's not fair..." In my motherly irritation, I just wonder... how did this all happen? I feel so blessed to see a new *harmattan* morning and my dry legs crying for a good helping of skin lotion. I am blessed to see that tiny tot in my church break free from her mother's arms and run across the room towards the pulpit just when Pastor is about to launch into the best part of his theological discourse- and smile to myself as the flustered usher attempts to catch the little fireball. I am blessed to see my aged Mother smile at me with crinkly eyes and say "hello, my golden girl..." And yes, there are the big things too that happen everyday, and sometimes I don't even see them until it's all over - escapes from death, healing from diseases, clearing up of debts, protection from the evil one and his schemes, visitation of angels, love of siblings and friends, the many unseen persons praying for me, release of resources when there was almost nothing...Do I know moments of sadness, sorrow and weakness? Yes, yes, yes. But STILL...His blessings overwhelm me.

"You anoint my head with oil; my cup runs over... Psalm 23:5b (NKJV)
"Blessed be the Lord, who daily loads us with benefits, the God of our salvation!" Psalm 68:19 (NKJV)

Are you counting your blessings with me? It will surprise you what the Lord does... everyday!

The Smile of God

Warm
Peaceful
Like the early morning sun
Peeping through the clouds
Is the smile of God.

Like leaves
Rustling in the wind
Delicate but strong
Beautiful
Is the smile of God.

Sweet
Heavenly
Like a symphony
On a still night
Is the smile of God.

Like waves
Touching the rocks
Of the sea shore
Gently, approvingly
Is the smile of God.

What would I give
For His smile?
He asks for nothing
But my heart.
So smile on me, my God.

19th April, 2010

The Brush of God

Wisps of clouds
Strewn across the skies
Background of the clearest blue
Light of the sun
Peeping through
Directing the paths of the clouds

A picture drawn
By an Unseen Hand
Spirals of unearthly paint
Stroking gently
In sweet contemplation
With human ingenuity flying across

A bird free and without care
Flapping its dancing wings
Claiming the glorious space
That God has made
What about a soul
Released to belong to the skies?

God's earth is beautiful
Contaminated or not
Only for a season
Creation groans
Waiting for the release
To sing Alleluias beyond the skies.

(An early summer day in 2010, sitting in a train from Reading to London and peering through the glass windows to observe the 'dancing wings' of a bird in the gloriously painted skies)

Reflections Twenty-two   December 9, 2007

Hannah!

Hannah! Her strength was in her mouth. Reading the story of Hannah in First Samuel Chapters 1 and 2 simply enthralls me. A childless wife in a patriarchal society with a rival who taunted her to distraction. Year after year her childlessness was used against her. Sounds familiar, right? Her only small comfort was a husband who loved her and tried not to complicate things more than they were. One day Hannah had had enough. So what did she do? She found her mouth! She turned her tears into **words** of supplication; [83] of specificity in asking for what she truly desired and of negotiation with none other but God; [84] and of faith and a certainty that her situation had changed even before the result was seen. [85] Boldness in trouble, boldness in anticipation, boldness when the result came, boldness in performing her part of the contract with God, and boldness in her praise! Have you read that story well? Did you notice how Hannah took her destiny into her own hands, placed it firmly in God's hands and did not wait for her husband? Did you notice how she responded to the male high priest who accused her of being drunk? [86] Did you notice how she took a *Nazarite* [87] vow on behalf of an unborn son she had not conceived before the Most High God? What about telling her husband when the child was born: "I will not go up until the child is weaned..." when the whole family had to show for the yearly feast? [88] And she *herself* taking the weaned Samuel to the house of the Lord in Shiloh, to serve as long as he lived, in fulfillment of her vow? [89] And what about the high praise of God in the mouth of a woman? Hear her:

"My heart rejoices in the LORD; my horn is exalted in the LORD. I smile at my enemies, because I rejoice in Your salvation..." 1Samuel 2:1 (NKJV)

Read on friends! Note the *power* of the words in her praise prayer. For a woman like me, oh, may God grant that I find my mouth in my generation, no matter the barriers. For with a mouth like Hannah's I can break through the strictures and barriers of culture, tradition or oppression of any form, in the name of Jesus! Amen!

Restful Prayer

It's a prayer said in anguish,
But it does not fret;
Resting in the hope
That the Father always hears.

It's a prayer poured out from the soul;
Deep, but is not anxious,
Believing that God's promises remain true
No matter how fiery the trial.

It's a prayer of sorrow and pain,
Lips moving, but not in vain;
Knowing that the Father sees
The extent of sorrow and depth of pain.

It's a shout, or a groan,
Or soundless prayer, not mere repetitions;
Believing that at the Throne of grace
Mercy is truly freely given.

It's a prayer of thanksgiving,
A heart warmed by the Father's love;
Knowing that He cares so much
His answer is sure – His will be done.

It's a prayer of laughter,
Of joy when a word is confirmed;
Of freedom like the blowing wind
Above and beyond what we ask or think.

O to pray like that,
Always knowing and trusting
That even silence is a gift
From the One who knows, sees and loves!

That He'll never fail His children;
That He knows what's always best;
That He'll always work for our good -
That is our hope, our peace and our rest!

16th May, 2010, at Leeds, UK

Two Women* [90]

One was a widow, the other well to do;
One lived in Zarapheth, the other in Shunnem;
One was ready to die; the other had no son;
God had prepared them both you see, for His surprise!

The prophet of God, sent to declare His word,
Approached the widow, most hopeless the situation;
Said to her, "give me a morsel of your food and drink" -
She didn't know, you see, she was chosen to do just that.

The other prophet of God passing by, reluctant even to rest,
Called in by the Shunnamite woman, to stay and to eat;
So he did, not knowing himself that God had him prepared
To release a blessing, a need he did not perceive.

What limits an all knowing, all loving God,
From preparing destinies ahead of two women;
Differentiated by status, space and motherhood;
Differentiated by race, class, need and time?

It's the all-seeing God who discriminates not;
God to whom belongs all who believe
And are ready to receive His convoluted surprises -
Ready with open hearts to take the step.

By destiny He destined them for blessings galore;
By choice they obeyed and received as planned;
One stepped out in faith to give her last morsel,
The other determined to serve, without thought to her trouble.

To the widow and her son, the jar of oil was never spent;
The bin of flour wasted not, all the days of her life on earth;
To the Shunnamite woman a living surprise of a son longed for;
Later and in addition, a beloved son, raised to life.

So it is that the Lord works, never His blessings to withhold
From those who uprightly walk, even in times of famine and lack;
He who looks upon a heart of obedience, an act of faith,
Always honors His word by prophet, king or angel, for always.

So these two women, united across time and space,
In the Lord, who created them to demonstrate His glory,
His love, His sacrifice, even Himself in different dimensions,
Do now, in the cloud of witnesses, urge us to do same.

That we might live in the light of His truth, what He says He does;
That we might live to obey His word; it never returns to Him void;
That we might live in expectation of His mercy, love and goodness;
That varied may be our experiences and seasons, but our God – He is One!

(*Inspired by the stories in 1st and 2nd Kings, of two women whose encounters with the prophets Elijah and Elisha at different times demonstrate the compassion and power of God in any situation.)

Reflections Twenty-three   December 4, 2007

Serving God?

I have been pondering about this matter. Why do I think when I'm doing something nice or good for another, that I am doing this in service to the Lord? I know, I know, that the Bible says so many things about being good to others; walking in good works; loving others and all of that. But somehow I am beginning to understand that the more you love God, the easier it becomes (or should become) to do these things and do them genuinely, because this is *fruit* you and I bear *as a result* of our relationship with Him... True, genuine service is a grace thing. What I'm trying to say is this; left to me alone, my being and doing good are nothing but a sham. Infact, I cannot serve God! That I am able to do good things and serve Him and others is a PRIVILEGE! That God allows me to do good things and even rewards me for them is a DOUBLE PRIVILEGE! Who am I to be among the throng of angels and saints who fall in worship before Him who sits on the Throne? Who am I that I can take a little child who is suffering neglect in my arms and embrace her with love? It is Jesus who grants me the privilege and enables me to demonstrate some of what He is to me and through me. It is His nature, and it is His work. I lay no claim to goodness. It is all His.

"And when He had opened the book, He found the place where it was written: "The Spirit of the Lord is upon Me, because He has anointed Me to preach the gospel to

the poor; He has sent Me to heal the brokenhearted..."
Luke 4: 17b-18 (NKJV)

Thank You Jesus, for allowing me into your vineyard to share in Your work. Please find me faithful. Thank You!

The Child on a Cross*

The Cross points me to God;
The Cross gives me to humanity;
Brings me to God for a relationship,
Gives me to humankind for community.

The test of my divinity is my humanity,
For receiving a child in Jesus' name
Is receiving the Christ Himself;
This is the crux, not for glory or fame.

Christ on the Cross, a child on a cross;
One suffering to save humankind,
The other suffering for humanity's cruelty;
Both are for and about me, both I must find.

I cannot claim that I know God
And ignore the child on a cross;
For my faith must show my works,
That I really know Christ on the Cross.

To You O Lord I pledge my life,
Not to walk in selfishness or naivety;
Pledge to serve with what You've given,
Remember that child like the Child of nativity.

That child for whom You came
To save, to redeem and to bless,
To see them through Your gentle eyes,
To love and receive too, no more no less.

(*Reflecting on the suffering of children from poverty, lack of love and care, abuse and exploitation. "A child on a cross", an expression I adopted from the title of a newsmagazine article I casually came across… and pondering my responsibility to those children as one who believes in the Christ who suffered for all humanity's sake)
15th May, 2010 at Leeds, UK

The Transfiguration* 91

There He stood
A Man, yet God
A cross between
The Law and the Prophets;
In Him both consists.
He is the Law;
He is the Prophets;
That is why
He alone, Christ
Can write the Law
Upon our hearts

And point the way
Of man to God;
For it is only
Through God
That one can come
To God.

There He stood
Completely changed;
Moses on His right,
Elijah on His left.
Yet in His glory,
He knew He had
His eyes upon
Peter, James and John
There at the foot
Of the mount;
Shining in light,
His heart was clearly
For those He came
To redeem and to save.
When they'd have stayed,
He gently turned them
Back to purpose.

"Time to go friends;
Time to descend
To the place
Where my heart belongs.
Though I'm from heaven,
I belong to earth
To bring heaven

To the hearts of earth,
And take the hearts
Back to the Father -
The Rest of humankind.
While there's light
Do not linger
Do not wait;
Moses and Elijah
Need you too."

"In the Father's plan
They are incomplete
Without you.
Come My friends -
Peter, James and John;
You are yet to become
What I purposed
You all to be;
This glory you see
Is for the here and now;
The greater glory
Is yet to come;
First by My rising,
Second by My coming
For the Law and Prophets
Must pass away,
Sealed by the Cross."

Peter said "Stay,"
James and John too;
But Christ said "No,
Down the mount we go."

So they followed,
Worked with the Master
Not understanding much -
Hard of hearing
Yet still followed
Until the day
The Son of God
Accomplished His purpose,
By the Cross of His death
And by His victory in rising;
Breathing upon them
The Breath of Transformation -
A foretaste of Transfiguration.

(Based on the accounts of the Transfiguration of Jesus in the Gospels of Matthew, Mark and Luke)
15th May, 2010 at Leeds, UK

Reflections Twenty-four   September 16, 2008

DON'T STOP!!

Whatever you are doing for the Lord, knowing that it is for the Lord, DON'T STOP! No matter what the devil is putting you through; no matter that it feels like a roller-coaster ride - one moment on your high hills, the next moment in the deep, deep valleys, DON'T STOP! God is honored by your tenacity of purpose, your determination to cling tightly to His robe and to persevere! Is it prayer for the saints? DON'T STOP! Is it visiting the sick and helpless? DON'T STOP! Is it writing poetry to His praise? DON'T STOP! Encouraging young people to choose purity? DON'T STOP!!

You see my dear friends, in one of those very low moments of my life when I felt nothing made sense any longer, it was these very words "DON'T STOP" from a dear Christian brother of mine that pulled me out of the doldrums and kept me going that day. Because of his encouragement I decided to keep writing and sharing my *Reflections*. Thank you, my brother. You don't know what those words mean to me! By His grace we receive strength to go on. No matter the testing or trial; no matter that is seems God is very far away, friends, do not faint, nor be weary.

"My grace is sufficient for you, for My strength is made perfect in weakness." I Corinthians 12:9 (NKJV)

I can't say this enough times-though it feels like the enemy is making deep furrows on your back, don't give up. Your labour will NEVER be in vain!

Grace

My eyes were cast down
Grace lifted them up once more

My body was broken
Grace mended it back together

My soul was shattered
Grace picked up the pieces and put it together

My strength was gone
Grace replaced it with more grace

My faith was dimmed
Grace shone its light on it again

My peace departed
Grace pulled it back to my breast

Then Grace called Mercy
And Mercy called Love
Together, they brought me back
To where I really, always belonged

In my Father's arms!

28th October, 2010

I Want to Dance

I want to dance again, Lord
Lose myself totally in Your love
Smile until my face simply aches
Laugh until my big belly rumbles...

I want to experience Your total freedom
Live a life that's full and funny
Play with children, walk bare feet
Dance all night till the morning light...

I want to feel the wind on my face
Hold a butterfly's tender wings
Run on the beach, wade in the waves
Dance to the beat of heaven's rhythms...

Everything that holds me bound
Today I let loose, let go, let fly
Nothing should hold me back, Lord
From being me, as You created me to be.

Dance, jump, twirl and clap
Laugh, smile, kiss and love
Weep, mourn when I have to
But still dancing in my heart.

So Lord, today I ask for a release
Of Your Spirit of freedom, of liberty
Let Him breathe anew all over me
The Spirit of the Lord, King of the Dance!

17th July, 2010

Reflections Twenty-Five   January 6, 2008

The More things Change...Flashback to New Year, 2008 [91]

"*The more things change, the more they remain the same...*" *so the saying goes.* I'm writing this in a brand New Year! In this season, may God be your mighty fortress and your defense. May He hide you under the shadow of His mighty wings, and give you a new song to sing this year. Say AMEN! I have heard the number 8 signifies new beginnings, and I believe that. Things are going to change this year - many things! In our lives, our families, our dreams, our work - many things. And I believe they will all work together for our good because the Bible says so. [93] Get ready and hang on tight for roller-coaster rides, zig- zags, about-turns, unexpected surprises, 'booms' (don't worry - good ones) - but also for challenges and opposition, because our adversary the devil will also be at work - full speed. But thanks be to God, who *always* leads us in triumph through Christ...[94] Therefore, we shall not be afraid, nor will we give up. So gird your loins! But you know what? The more things change, **one thing** will never change for me - no matter what! **Hear what the Lord God says:**

"For the mountains shall depart (crumble), and the hills be removed (shaken), but My kindness (unfailing love) shall not depart from you (will never end); nor shall my covenant of peace (and completeness) be removed." <u>*Says the Lord*</u> *who has mercy (compassion and love)*

for you."Isaiah 54:10 (my combination of Translations from NKJV and the Amplified Bible)

What sweet comfort! What constancy! What faithfulness! As Project 2008, **fix** your eyes on Jesus, for His love for you changes not. Never ever.

Today*

Today, I learnt that
Miracles are made in the middle of storms;
Waiting for God to act means just that –
Waiting.

Today, I learnt that
God makes heroines out of
Messed lives,
Messed minds,
Messed bodies…

Today, I learnt that
God is with me,
When no one is for me;
Giving up is not an option,
Because angels are on their way…

Today, I learnt that
There are remarkable people,
With remarkable stories;

I don't have to look hard –
They're right next to me…

Today, I learnt that
Life's not a coincidence,
When God is weaving His tapestry;
He brings people across my way
Who are miracles made in storms…

(*The Poem is a contemplation on life's surprises. Two years before, the New Year had started with hope and enthusiasm. I learnt as the year progressed, that we don't always get the good things we project, and often, we underrate the opposition and challenges, and the strength we need to withstand such. But I also learnt in my wilderness experience with OCD that God really, truly, does not change. He's constant in His truth, faithfulness and the outworking of good in the lives of His children. Miracles are truly made in storms, and I am a living testimony of this.)
10th March, 2010

Flowers in Stony Places

The courts of the Lord
Are made with stone
Yet He plants His own
Flowers, in stony places.

Flowers blossom today
Tomorrow they are gone
Fading away with the wind
And heat, rain and storm.

But the flowers of the Lord
Planted in His courts
Fixed in stony cracks
Flourish in His house.

Come wind or rain
Come storm or fire
In surprising places
Are flowers among stones.

Faithful is the Lord
Who plants His own
In between cracks of stone
To bring to full bloom.

Forever they last
Watered by invisible hands
Weathering changing seasons
Emitting their fragrance.

The stones give character
To the fragile flower
Not to crush or destroy
But to shape and give strength.

Beautiful blooms are we
Rooted, grounded therein
His love, though oft seems
The stones so hard, surround.

Flowers in stony places
A planting of the Lord

Is the story of the child
Belonging to God.

15th August, 2010

Closing Poem

The Wilderness of Hope!

You spared my life
So many times, so many ways;
I did not deserve to live,
No, I did not think so.
But the great God of Horeb, [96]
The I Am that I Am,
Utterly Transcendent God
Would tolerate one like me;
Because there came a time, you see,
I thought, "Woe is me, my life is gone."

I know I got saved;
Always believed I had You
The day I said yes;
Lord here I come to You -
"Naked come to You for dress;
Helpless look to You for grace;
Foul I to the fountain fly;
Wash me Savior or I'll die."*
Your word is true and sure You did,
For whosoever will, may come. [97]
There was I, asking for salvation
My sins blotted out by the Blood;
I had no fear, joy was mine.

Then one day from no where
Or so it did seem to me,
A terrible thought flew through my mind,

Then came, "You are a blasphemer;
You have fallen from grace.
Your great God is terrible;
You have no plea, no case.
The thought took a deadly grip;
More thoughts did follow in rapid succession -
Surely the Holy Spirit must be grieved
Surely I had sinned the unpardonable sin.

Terrible thoughts, dark thoughts;
The light in me I could not find.
Plagued I was, and in great distress.
I tossed, I turned, and burned;
Literally felt I was in a kind of hell.
"Mercy, Lord!" I cried and cried;
My wounded soul just would not
Accept that I had already been ransomed-
Saved by the Blood of the Savior's Cross.

I pined, dried up and wasted away
Unknown terrors gripped my mind;
The enemy whispered deadly lies.
I felt so weary, felt I had died;
But all the time something prodded my heart.
"Mercy, Lord!" My soul cried time after time;
What is this, where do I stand?
Why do I feel, all's out of hand?

Obsessive, intrusive, uncontrollable thoughts,
Came and went, teased and taunted;
You're done, you're gone, and you'll die
Without hope and without mercy.

But my soul would cry out, "Mercy, Lord!
Come through for me, You're all I have;
Come through Savior, or I'll die;
Do not cast me out into utter darkness.

It was so hard, it was so painful;
I couldn't understand it, neither handle;
I did not know the enemy was at work
To make me believe the deadliest lies.
He had cast a spell on my brain;
Unwired it, in a sense to make me think
That my God had forsaken me, He was gone;
He didn't love me, not anymore.
Who could I tell, who would understand
How someone like me could fall so hard?

Was it a test, a trial or a temptation?
I did not know, I could not tell -
A combination of all three I suppose,
For I know now that God heard my every plea.
Persecuted I was, but not forsaken;
Struck down, but not destroyed; [98]
Completely perplexed and in great distress
But never forgotten, never lost.

The more the enemy tried to destroy.
The more God loved, more and more.
Reached me He did in total darkness;
Somewhere far in the recesses of my spirit;
For that is His candle, His way to commune
That I'll not die, but live to declare His works.
It took a long time, many months

To climb out of that hell hole I must say;
The foundations had been chipped and damaged;
It took God's love to make the righteous stand.

Many discoveries have I made on the way;
Many lessons, both joyful and sad.
I learned great men and women of faith
Had been sold those same kind of lies;
Lies to lead to depression, obsession, even death -
An experience common to humankind;
When I thought that I alone
Had such ill fortune befall my soul.
Those great people lived to tell their stories
Of God's grace abounding, love abiding.

Analyze all I could, I couldn't tell why;
A combination of factors may be the cause.
But God's unfathomable ways remain;
His sovereignty is unchallenged, He knows it all.
"His purposes will ripen fast,
Unfolding every hour," Cowper sang*
A giant in the Lord who went through a kind,
Survived to write that famous song
That Christians sing to praise the Lord,
To acknowledge all His perfect ways.

Surely His redemption is sure;
The Enemy can never outwit Him.
Once God has said "YOU ARE MINE", [99]
He makes it His cause to deliver and save.
Depression, obsession, spasms and all,
He took me out, gently, unobtrusively.

Thoughts of God

I can't even tell when I started getting well -
When cries of mercy turned into song.
Once the silence was broken prayer went up;
Watchmen He stationed all over my walls.

What a Savior, what a Friend
What a Deliverer, what a God!
Nothing hidden, nothing surprising,
He knows the enemy, tricks and all.
I am still walking the road to wellness,
Wholeness, rest and restoration.
My mind once a while does wander and stray-
I ask "Are You still here, dear God?
Hold me fast, never let me go,
You brought me this far; grace take me home;
Home one day to be with the Lord,
When my work is finished, assignment done."

And this story I have to tell,
And truly tell it very well.
The children of God must become shrewd;
And never ignorant of the enemy's deceits.
He comes to steal, kill and destroy;
But Christ is ours to heal, save and restore.
Patience is required and strong trust;
One thing's for sure – God's faithfulness.

So "this is my story, this is my song;
Praising my Savior, all the day long".*
This mouth I won't shut till the day is done;
I will tell of Your works of love and power.
Hell cannot stop You, darkness will flee;

Nothing can stop God on a rescue mission.
No matter the depth of despair, sin or shame,
Our God is able, Our God will save.
Our defense will defend His own;
Keeping us, mind, body, spirit and soul.

So what's the lesson, what's the gain?
My life I pledge to serve through this pain;
Many are wounded, weeping in Zion,
All they need is an understanding heart;
One who'll come alongside and say "It is well",
The struggle will end, the darkness will turn;
You are not alone, I'm here, sent
To give the comfort the Godhead gave.[100]
For there is a reason, there is a work,
It'll ne'er be in vain –Alleluia –
The name of the Lord be praised!

(*The phrase comes from the famous hymn titled "Rock of Ages, Cleft for me", by Augustus Montague Toplady, 1740-78; * William Cowper, 1731-1800, wrote the hymn "God moves in a mysterious way." Part of the 5th verse of the hymn is quoted above; *The refrain 'This is my story, this is song' is from the hymn "Blessed Assurance" written by Frances Jane van Alstyne, 1820-1915)

END NOTES

1. Psalm 138:2c
2. Isaiah 42:8; Isaiah 48:11b
3. Philippians 2:13
4. See Luke 12:37
5. Isaiah 42:14
6. Isaiah 43:1a – b; Isaiah 44: 22b
7. Jeremiah 29:11
8. Jeremiah 31: 3a
9. John 17:11;16
10. Warren, R. (2002), *The Purpose Driven Life*. Zondervan, Grand Rapids, Michigan (and Oasis International Limited)
11. Songs of Solomon 2:46
12. Isaiah 54:10
13. Revelation 1:14b;15
14. Psalm 144: 1
15. Exodus 15:1
16. Proverbs 18:10
17. Isaiah 54:15
18. Genesis 15:6; Isaiah 41:8; James 2:23

19. Genesis 12:10–20. A similar incident happened in Genesis 20: 1–18
20. Genesis 22:2-10
21. Genesis 14:14
22. Philippians 2:13
23. Genesis 12:10-20; Genesis 20:1-18
24. The story is found in Genesis 16
25. Genesis 14
26. I used the expression 'finding faith' because obsessive-compulsive disorder (OCD), especially religious OCD and scrupulosity as a condition attacks one's faith, creating severe self-doubt and doubts about one's identity in God. OCD has been described as the 'doubting disease' by some experts. See for e.g., Ciarrocchi, J.W. (1995), *The Doubting Disease: Help for Scrupulosity and Religious Compulsions*. Integration Books, USA
27. Isaiah 40:29-30
28. The *Poem* is titled "Triple Jeopardy" because in John 11, Lazarus went through three stages of trouble – falling sick, dying, and being buried – before Jesus came and reversed the situation, raising him from the dead.
29. Genesis 37:24
30. Jeremiah 33:1-3
31. Daniel 6:16
32. Ruth 2:2-23
33. Exodus 3:14. God commands Moses to tell the children of Israel, the in captivity in Egypt that "I AM" has sent him to deliver them from bondage to Pharaoh. In

the notes of the New King James Version (NKJV) of the Ryrie Study Bible, (pg. 95) "I AM WHO I AM" is said to be the inner meaning of 'Yahweh' – "I am the One who is", emphasizing God's dynamic and active self-existence.
34. Psalm 84:6. Baca is from the root meaning 'to weep', or a valley of desolation. See NKJV, Ryrie Study Bible notes on pg. 889
35. Deuteronomy 33:27
36. Exodus 3
37. 1 Samuel 16
38. Numbers 22:27-31
39. 1 Samuel 1
40. Luke 1:26-56
41. Mark 12:42
42. John 4:1-42
43. Matthew 19:14-15; Mark 9:36-37
44. Luke 19:2-10
45. Luke 6:20; Matthew 5:3
46. Luke 2:7
47. Matthew 27:31-56; Mark 15:21-41; Luke 23:26-49; John 19:17-37
48. 1 Corinthians 1:18
49. 1 Corinthians 1:18
50. Isaiah 49:...
51. Proverbs 18:10
52. Tozer, A.W. (1982), *The Pursuit of God*. Christian Publications
53. 1 Samuel 2:9c
54. Zechariah 4:6b
55. Genesis 15:16

56. The promise of God to save and deliver His people is found in several passages of scripture. See e.g., Psalm 91:15; Daniel 3:17; 2 Timothy 4:18; 2 Peter 2:9; Hebrews 7:25.
57. Philippians 2:13
58. Jeremiah 29:11
59. Romans 8:29
60. Jeremiah 3:22
61. Jeremiah 31:33c
62. Numbers 6:25-26
63. Matthew 17:20, Luke 17:6. Jesus urges His disciples in these verses to exercise whatever level of faith they have in God, even if it is 'mustard seed' faith.
64. Matthew 11:30
65. Joshua 10:12-13
66. Isaiah 53:4
67. Psalm 23:6a
68. Psalm 18:35c
69. Deuteronomy 33:26 "There is no one like the God of Jeshurun, who rides the heavens to help you, and in His excellency on the clouds..."
70. Marion Jones was a world champion track and field athlete. She won five medals at the 2000 summer Olympics in Sydney, Australia. She agreed to forfeit all her medals and prizes after admitting that she took performance enhancement drugs (steroids), See http://en.wikipedia.org/wiki/Marion_Jones
71. Psalm 22:1a; Matthew 27:46; Mark 15:34

72. Revelation 5:5
73. Psalm 50:10b
74. See Psalm 18:7-14. One glimpses from these verses the awesome power and greatness of God.
75. See Zechariah 4:96
76. Numbers 23:24 says "Look, a people rises like a lioness and lifts itself like a lion..."
77. Psalm 32:2a
78. John 1:29. Also Revelation 5, 12, 13 and 19 all mention the "Lamb that was slain..."
79. Isaiah 66:1
80. Ephesians 1:21
81. Psalm 68:20
82. 1 Peter 3:19
83. 1 Samuel 1:10
84. 1 Samuel 1:11
85. 1 Samuel1:18b
86. 1Samuel 1:13-14
87. 1 Samuel 1:11d. A *Nazarite*, from a verb meaning 'to separate or abstain', was a layperson of either sex who was bound by a vow of consecration to God's service for a specified period of time or for life. He/she could not cut his/her hair, drink wine or defile him/herself by going near a dead person. See NKJV of the Ryrie Study Bible notes, pg. 216.
88. 1 Samuel 1:22
89. 1 Samuel 1: 24-28
90. The *Poem* is based on two stories; (a) the account of the Prophet Elijah's encounter

with a widow who lived in Zarapheth (1 Kings 8: 16-24); (b) the account of the Prophet Elisha's encounter with a woman who lived in Shunem (2 Kings 4:8-37).
91. Matthew 17:1-8; Mark 9:2-8; Luke 9:28-36
92. In the New Year of 2008, I was full of optimism, enthusiasm, boundless energy, and looking forward to a year of excitement, favor and joy. The *Reflection* I wrote depicted my optimistic outlook for the year. However, in May 2008, I started experiencing the first frightening symptoms of OCD, which I knew next to nothing about. By the end of 2008, I was in the throes of a deep, dark depression. Praise the Lord, by December 2009, I had clear signals that I was beginning to recover from the disorder and its accompanying illnesses. The quote from Isaiah 54:10 became one of my favorites of the several Bible verses that gave me hope over and over again in a time of dryness, doubt and bewilderment.
93. Romans 8:28
94. 2 Corinthians 2:14
95. The title of this *Poem*, 'Flowers in Stony Places', is adopted from the title of a romantic novel I read in my teen years written by Majorie Lewty, and published by Mills and Boon in 1975
96. Exodus 3:1c. *Horeb* is another name for Mt. Sinai, described as the mountain of God in this Bible verse. This is where God Almighty

appeared to Moses in a flame of fire from the midst of a bush which burned but was miraculously not consumed. (Exodus 3: 2).
97. John 3:15-16; 36
98. 2 Corinthians 4:9
99. Isaiah 43:1b
100. 1 Corinthians 1:3-4

APPENDIX ONE

What is Obsessive Compulsive Disorder (OCD)?

OCD is described as a distressing bio-medical, neuro-psychiatric condition (Osborn, 2008; Schwartz, 1997), characterized by obsessions and compulsions. The obsessions are usually persistent, recurrent thoughts, images or impulses that are experienced by the sufferer as repulsive, inappropriate and intrusive. These are not ordinary, everyday excessive worries about life or circumstances, but thoughts and/or mental images that result in marked anxiety and distress. The person suffering from obsessional thoughts, impulses or images tries in vain to suppress, neutralize or ignore them with some other thought or action. These vain attempts to suppress or neutralize the thoughts or images result in repetitive behaviors, (e.g., excessive hand washing or checking of locked doors), or mental acts (e.g., repeating words silently, praying, excessive confession of sins) which one does in response to the obsessive thoughts or images.

OCD causes such anxiety and distress that it significantly interferes with a person's normal routine, social activities and occupational functioning, especially when one does not know or understand the nature of the condition. OCD often results in depression and its attendant psychosomatic symptoms, such as suicide ideation, helplessness and hopelessness, nightmares, weight loss, bodily aches, crawling skin sensations and many others.

It has been discovered after many years of research that OCD is caused by what is described as a "lock" or "glitch" in the brain, causing a chemical imbalance (Schwartz, 1997, Osborn, 2008). Its root cause is not totally understood although it has been traced to certain factors including genetic factors, a particular bacteria causing agent, and environmental stressors. OCD affects an estimated 4 million adults in the USA and 2-3% of the population of the UK. I have not come across much information on OCD statistics and facts in sub-Saharan Africa. After many years of painstaking work, OCD is deemed treatable primarily through Cognitive Behavioral Treatment (CBT), particularly Exposure Response Prevention (ERP) therapy, oftentimes in combination with medication.

When is OCD described as Scrupulosity?

Scrupulosity is a term given in Christian circles to the OCD condition in people whose obsessions are primarily unwanted, repulsive images, thoughts or urges that are completely antithetical to their religious beliefs. The thoughts are characterized by excessive doubts, sacrilegious images, blasphemous thoughts and the like that are most bewildering, especially to a believer. The sufferer usually tries to get rid of the thoughts or images without much success, because the more one tries to suppress them, the more they occur. The person then gets into compulsions such as constantly seeking assurances about their salvation, or making excessive confessions to God for forgiveness (e.g., saying the sinner's prayer many times over). The 17th Century writer and preacher, John Bunyan, chronicles his experience of this condition (though not known as OCD at the time) in his classic book "Grace Abounding to the Chief of Sinners."

My thoughts on how the Christian community/ Church can help:

Pastors and counselors in the Christian community need to expand their knowledge of mental health conditions generally, because ignorance can lead to causing further harm and distress to one who already suffers from a "wounded conscience." OCD in particular is an extremely distressing condition for a believer because of the nature of the attack. I have no doubt about its spiritual underpinnings as a deadly attack from the enemy of our souls and the accuser of the brethren. However, lack of knowledge about this condition may lead to reinforcing the repetitive, cyclical nature of the condition by the Pastor or counselor who thinks he/she is helping by constantly re-assuring the sufferer concerning their doubts and fears. Blaming the sufferer for the condition, accusing them of not having enough faith, or ordering them to 'set your life right' only serve to increase the anguish and guilt of the sufferer. Also taking the sufferer through endless deliverance sessions or ritualistic prayers may not be the answer to OCD. I simply put it this way – for the scrupulous/OCD sufferer, the enemy came, touched one's brain and left, leaving the brain to do his dirty work of bringing unwanted thoughts, images, doubts, fears and severe suffering. Deliverance may help, but whoever you are casting out may not be there at all. Rather, knowledge, empathy and understanding, constructive use of scripture, prayer, guidance and appropriate referral to a mental health expert may be more helpful. Especially for women, this is of grave concern to me not because men suffer less, but because OCD's attendant miseries – anxiety, depression, panic attacks, palpitations, nightmares, distorted patterns of thinking etc, mimic symptoms associated with hormonal changes during post-partum, peri-menopause or menopause stages. Particular attention must be paid to women complaining of such symptoms since OCD or some other generalized anxiety disorder may be present or occurring, so that the appropriate counseling and support can be given.

My thoughts on how the Mental Health Community in Ghana can help:

There isn't much on OCD prevalence, facts or statistics in Ghana. I am inclined to believe that due to the presenting symptoms in our cultural setting, OCD is being misdiagnosed. The concern is deepened by the fact that there are not enough mental health professionals to serve the current population and those requiring mental health services. Many people consult Pastors and herbal/traditional medicine practitioners rather than psychiatric/clinical psychology professionals because of belief systems, stigma, and general inadequate access to mental health facilities in our country. Below are some of my thoughts on how the mental health community can help:

- Form collaborative partnerships with international research institutions to conduct countrywide studies into OCD and other anxiety disorders
- Collaborate with the media to educate the public on mental health issues generally and how to seek and get appropriate help
- Train more mental health practitioners for services delivery at the community level
- Conduct more extensive enquiry into clients' presenting symptoms and use the appropriate tools (such as administering OCD tests if suspected) before reaching diagnosis

- Collaborate with the Church and other faith-based groups in education, identification of symptoms, counseling approaches and referrals
- Christian mental health professionals should collaborate with each other and educate the Christian community on the Christian perspectives of mental health, with a special focus on particularly vulnerable populations (women, children, the aged and homeless).

My thoughts on what Christian OCD sufferers can do:

- Do not suffer in silence. Tell a trusted friend, counselor or professional
- Do not be afraid to learn about your particular symptoms – find out more
- Don't wait until the condition gets out of control. See a mental health practitioner the moment you perceive your thoughts are not well ordered or controllable
- Remember that you are not alone! As the Bible says, your Christian brothers and sisters may be going through the same kind of trial. (I Cor 10:13) This is true. You are not what the enemy is whispering into your mind!
- When doubts and fears about your identity as a child of God come to you, cling tightly to what you have known and believed before – that you are a child of God, that Jesus died for you, that your sins are truly

forgiven, that grace is still present and working, that God says He will never leave you nor forsake you, that you will gain freedom from oppression. Say them to yourself. Hold on to promise passages in the Word of God, NO MATTER WHAT YOU ARE FEELING. ALL KINDS OF NEGATIVE AND STRANGE FEELINGS WILL COME TO YOU, BUT REMEMBER, FAITH IS NOT A FEELING. SAY AND AFFIRM TO YOURSELF WHAT YOU KNOW AND HAVE BELIEVED EVEN IF YOU DON'T *FEEL* THEY ARE TRUE OF YOU.
- Journal your progress – you will be amazed what God can and will do on this journey!
- Finally, "in patience, possess your souls." It takes time, and support. Hang in there. With good counseling, medication if necessary, prayer and support from friends and family, and with JESUS, you'll come through it!

Do you need a friend because no one understands you? E-mail me at adaboagye2@gmail.com.

APPENDIX TWO

Helpful Resources and Websites

Books*

- Bunyan, J. (1666), *Grace Abounding to the Chief of Sinners.* (Modernized Version, 2000). Evangelical Press, USA
- Ciarrocchi, J. W. (1993), *A Minister's Handbook of Mental Disorders.* Integration Books, USA
- Ciarrocchi, J.W. (1995), *The Doubting Disease: Help for Scrupulosity and Religious Compulsions.* Integration Books, USA
- Schwartz, J. (1997), *Brain Lock: Free Yourself from Obsessive-Compulsive Behavior.* Harper Collins, USA
- Osborn, I. (2008) *Can Christianity Cure Obsessive Compulsive Disorder?* Brazos Press – A Division of Baker Publishing Group.

Recommended Websites

www.ocfoundation.org
www.ocdaction.org.uk
www.ocdhope.com
www.ocdawareness.com
www.cherryPedrick.com
www.ocdchicago.org
www.mhsource.com
www.ocdonline.com
www.aabt.org
www.mentalhealth.com
www.psyhcentral.com
www.healthyplace.com/communities/ocd/doubt

*There are several other good books. The above listed are those I have read so far.

APPENDIX THREE

- For a profile of John Bunyan, see en.wikipedia.org/wiki/John_Bunyan.
- For a detailed account of his experience of OCD/Scrupulosity, read his autobiography "Bunyan, J. (1666), *Grace Abounding to the Chief of Sinners.* (Modernized Version, 2000). Evangelical Press, USA
- For a profile of Martin Luther, the initiator of the Protestant Reformation, see en.wikipedia.org/wiki/Martin_Luther. For a detailed study of Luther's struggle with obsessive thinking, see Erik H. Erickson, *Young Man Luther, A Study in Psychoanalysis and History* (New York: W.W Norton, 1962)
- For a profile of St. Therese of Lisiuex, also known as 'Little Flower', see en.wikipedia.org/wiki/Therese-of-lisieux
- Other well-known OCD (and related disorders) sufferers include Samuel Johnson (en.wikipedia.org/wiki/Samuel_Johnson); St.

Jane Chantal (http://wau.org/resources/article/saint_Jane_de_Chantal_15721641/); St Ignatius Loyola (en.wikipedia.org/wiki/Ignatius_of_Loyola)
- For well-known Christians known to have suffered major depression, read about William Cowper (en.wikipedia.org/wiki/William_Cowper); Charles H. Spurgeon (en.wikipedia.org/wiki/Charles_Spugeon). See also Spurgeon's article "When a Preacher is Downcast" at www.gotothebible.com/HTML/downcast.html
- For an excellent analysis of Luther, Bunyan and St. Therese's experience with OCD as a psychological affliction, read Dr. Ian Osborn's *"Can Christianity Cure Obsessive-Compulsive Disorder?* (2008) Brazos Press

Lightning Source UK Ltd.
Milton Keynes UK
173892UK00002B/2/P